DEPARTMENT OF THE ENVIRONMENT

Derelict Land Prevention and the Planning System

Final Report

Arup Economics & Planning
13 Fitzroy Street
LONDON W1P 6BQ
Tel: 0171–465 3965
Fax: 0171–465 3677

in association with
Clark Whitehill
Berwin Leighton

London: HMSO

Contents

Appendices

Preface

The report was commissioned by the Department of the Environment in July 1994 from Arup Economics & Planning. The majority of the work was carried out by Corinne Swain, David Wickens, Jeroen Weimar and Gwilym Jones, with case study inputs from Lorna Andrews and Jim Strike. Specialist legal advice was provided by Berwin Leighton (Ian Trehearne) and taxation advice by Clark Whitehill (Chris Sales).

The study team were supported by a Steering Group whose guidance and technical inputs are gratefully acknowledged. The Steering Group comprised:

Lillian P. H. Birch (Chairman)	Department of the Environment (PD3D)
Alastair Bishop	Department of the Environment (PD3D)
Ann Ward	Department of the Environment (PD2C)
Judith Denner	Department of the Environment (CLL)
Simon Lait	Department of the Environment (LPD)
Jeremy Bayliss	Chairman of the CBI Land Use Panel
Richard Bradley	English Partnerships
Tom Hardie	Scottish Office.

We also acknowledge the assistance given by the many people who participated in the interview and case study stages of the project.

This report's findings, conclusions and recommendations represent the views of Arup Economics and Planning, and do not necessarily represent the views of Steering Group members or the Secretary of State.

EXECUTIVE SUMMARY

Background

1   The concept of restoration is firmly established in the handling of applications for mineral extraction. However, with minor exceptions for particular types of development, consideration is not explicitly given to ensuring that a site is left in a state capable of re-use when giving planning permission for built development.

2   The purpose of this research has been to follow up the Government's consultation exercise (*Proposals to Prevent Land from Becoming Derelict, February 1992*), and to examine the ways in which the planning system might be used to prevent non-mineral sites from becoming derelict in the future.

3   This study has been undertaken by Arup Economics & Planning in four main stages between July 1994 and February 1995.

Existing Mechanisms to Influence the Future Use and Condition of Sites

4   Existing planning mechanisms to deal with derelict land are largely <u>reactive</u> rather than proactive. They deal with the problem of inherited dereliction (the stock of existing derelict land) rather than preventing the occurrence of derelict land in the future (reducing the flow of new land becoming derelict). Existing planning mechanisms include the following default powers:

*   S.215 Notices (S.215 Town and Country Planning Act 1990) to require steps to be taken by the owner/ occupier of a site to remedy the situation where issues of amenity are threatened.

*   Repairs Notices (S.48 Planning (Listed Buildings and Conservation Areas) Act 1990) to secure works to preserve a listed building from deteriorating or falling into disrepair.

*   Dangerous Structures Notices (S.77 Building Act 1984) to secure works of repair or restoration or, should the owner elect, demolition of a building or structure which is dangerous.

5   The current tax system does not provide a fiscal penalty on the holding of land in a derelict state. Neither does it provide any tax incentive to undertake rehabilitation works, except in relation to the restoration of mineral extraction sites (S.109 of the Capital Allowances Act 1990).

6   Planning policies and associated grant regimes promote the regeneration of derelict sites. Although the normal operation of the development market recycles some derelict land, it is largely central and local government which assist in bringing significantly damaged land back into productive use. Public/private sector partnerships are a favoured vehicle.

7 Other mechanisms which can influence the condition that a site is left in following completion of operations are:

- waste management controls which include provision for certificates of completion relating to the handover of landfill sites

- industry codes of practice, some of which encourage members to clear sites on decommissioning

- Environmental Assessment mechanisms which have encouraged the implications of decommissioning to be considered at the project planning stage

- leasehold agreements which can include conditions requiring the lessee to return the site to the lessor in its original condition on its expiry of the lease.

Prevention of Future Dereliction

8 The primary objective of this study has been to look at practical ways that might reduce the <u>flow</u> of new land becoming derelict and in addition help to reduce costs borne by the public purse. The emphasis is therefore on prevention. This would shift the burden of leaving sites in a state capable of re-use onto the landowner or occupier. This is line with the 'polluter pays principle', as formalised in the Environmental Protection Act 1990. The provisions of this Act together with the current Environment Bill should reduce the risks of ground contamination from any new development, and will thereby assist the prevention of derelict land in the future.

9 Mechanisms investigated in this study are largely those that can be delivered by the planning system, particularly through the development control process. Associated fiscal measures have also been considered. Examples of fiscal measures used in other developed countries to encourage site rehabilitation and/or prevent future dereliction are summarised in the main report.

10 In order to prevent dereliction an attempt must be made to foresee and seek to control the sets of circumstances that may give rise to land becoming derelict. The types of development likely to pose most risk of future dereliction are:

(i) temporary buildings or structures with no practical alternative use, particularly where there is rapid technological change, eg in telecommunications and some forms of power generation;

(ii) industrial activities involving specialist structures with no practical alternative use, eg petro-chemicals, the water, gas and medical waste disposal industries;

(iii) development in rural areas where alternative planning policy constraints restrict acceptable alternative uses, eg military establishments, prisons, hospitals, theme parks and all weather leisure facilities.

Options Considered

11 Five main options have been considered in this study. Two of these equate with the options put forward in the 1992 Consultation Paper, and relate specifically to aspects of the planning system. A third option combines financial measures with one of these planning controls. The remaining two options are financial measures, which might be used in general support of planning objectives.

12 Various key issues have been explored which need to be resolved in order to identify a workable proposition for each option. These issues can be summarised as:

Rehabilitation Conditions	Definition of required rehabilitation standards
	Definition of types of development where conditions may be appropriate
	Legitimate forms of conditions (compatible with Circular 1/85)
Financial Guarantees	Determining the amount of guarantee
	Determining the trigger point for release
	Most appropriate sources of finance

Extending Local	Limitations of existing S.215 powers
	Authority Powers Defining type of new provision
	Basis and level of cost recovery
	Trigger mechanisms for action
Tax Relief on Rehabilitation Expenditure	Incentive mechanisms
Tax on Holding Derelict Land	Method of tax assessment
	Basis of levying charges
	Distinguishing between vacant and derelict land

13   In exploring the potential mechanics of the five options, several variants were identified. Only the strongest candidates were taken forward to the evaluation stage. Five variants were rejected as being not sufficiently focused on derelict land prevention and because they were unlikely to be feasible. These were:

- imposing rehabilitation conditions on all types of built development (but leaving the option open to apply them where circumstances would make them feasible);

- using insurance-based schemes or industry funds to provide financial guarantees;

- extending CPO powers to bring more derelict land into the public sector;

- providing tax incentives for developers to redevelop derelict land;

- earmarking revenue from a potential tax on the holding of derelict land to contribute to the costs of reclaiming the existing stock of derelict land (hypothecation).

Evaluating the Effectiveness of the Options

14   The five options which provide mechanisms to assist derelict land prevention have been systematically evaluated against six criteria. The evaluation was based on professional judgement informed by the opinions put forward by organisations interviewed and the case study work undertaken. A qualitative rather than quantitative assessment has been undertaken due to the complexity of the subject matter. A comparative table in the main report describes the main implications of each of the options. The results are summarised below.

COMPARATIVE EVALUATION

	Rehab. Conditions	Financial Guarantees	New LA Power	Tax Relief	Tax
Impact	✔				(✔)
Practicality	✔		✔	✔	
Incentive		✔			✔
Flexibility	✔	✔	✔	✔	✔
Does Not Deter Investment	(✔)			✔	
No Call on Public Funds		✔			(✔)
Minimal Legislative Change	✔	✔		✔	

15   The most effective option in terms of **impact** was found to be the use of rehabilitation conditions, since this is a proactive mechanism targeted specifically on preventing land from becoming derelict. However, its effectiveness would only be felt in the medium to long term. A tax on the holding of derelict land would also provide an effective deterrent which could encourage land to be held in a vacant state rather than a derelict state, in areas or periods of low market demand for redevelopment. The overall effects of the three remaining options would be more limited.

16   Three of the five options were judged to be **practical**, namely rehabilitation conditions, a new S.215 type power, and tax relief on rehabilitation expenditure. There would be constraints in terms of implementing a system of financial guarantees to back rehabilitation conditions at the current time, and severe constraints on introducing a tax on the holding of derelict land.

17   The reverse situation would exist in relation to the degree of **incentive** provided to landowners to prevent dereliction. Financial guarantees and a tax on the holding of derelict land would provide the greatest incentive, while the effects of the other three options would be more limited.

18   All five options would be capable of being implemented in such a way that they were **flexible** to local circumstances.

19   Tax relief on rehabilitation expenditure would have little or no impact as a **deterrent to investment**. The effect of rehabilitation conditions would also be limited. The effect of a new S.215 type power is uncertain but would depend on the track record of particular authorities. The remaining two options could have a potentially significant effect on deterring investment.

20   Two options would have only limited effects on the demand for **public funds**, namely rehabilitation conditions and financial guarantees. There would be an unknown loss of tax revenue should tax relief be allowed on rehabilitation expenditure; this may be small but it needs further research. A potentially high demand could be created by a new S.215 type power but would be dependent on its success at cost recovery. The costs of implementing a tax on the holding of derelict land should be offset by additional revenues.

21   Three of the options would require limited **legislative change**. This would favourably influence the speed at which they could be introduced. A new S.215 type power would require a new provision to the Town and Country Planning Act. The introduction of a tax on the holding of derelict land would require a change in fiscal policy, as well as new legislation, and might be perceived as running counter to existing principles of property rights.

Conclusions

22   The growing acceptance of the 'polluter pays principle' and of the imperatives of sustainable development makes the timing right to consider introducing the concept of rehabilitation of sites more widely into the control of development. The starting point for any mechanism to be effective should be to promote an approach which will change the climate of opinion about the use of land following the closure of an operation, and which will help landowners, operators and occupiers to be more aware of their stewardship role.

23   The three options with the most potential to prevent land from becoming derelict and which do not appear to have any overriding practical or political constraints to their implementation are:

- rehabilitation conditions on certain types of activities
- a new S.215 type provision
- carry-back provisions to provide tax relief on rehabilitation expenditure.

24   These mechanisms are not mutually exclusive. Each works in a different way and would be focused on a different aspect of preventing land from becoming derelict. The implementation of each of these mechanisms would be complementary and mutually reinforcing.

Recommendations

Climate of Opinion

1 Government should issue guidance on the use of the planning system to prevent land becoming derelict (eg a redraft of PPG1 and/or PPG12). If new legislation is introduced (see recommendation 13), a Circular on derelict land prevention would assist understanding of the legislation and provide a reminder of existing mechanisms.

2 Local authorities should be encouraged to discuss rehabilitation/reuse implications of development with applicants at the planning application stage, especially for greenfield development.

3 Operators/occupiers should be encouraged to consider it part of their responsibility to the community to provide the tidying up of sites and making suitable for alternative use, rather than abandonment when their use ends (this applies particularly where technology and demand patterns change rapidly and development occurs on a greenfield site).

4 Relevant industry groups, particularly in older industries (eg chemical, petroleum, steel) should be encouraged to adopt rehabilitation practices and instill a stronger environmental conscience through industry codes of practice or conduct.

Rehabilitation Conditions

5 A wider use of rehabilitation conditions should be encouraged within current legislation and practice for time-limited developments, such as windfarms, telecommunications masts.

6 The use of rehabilitation conditions should be extended over time to specified types of development, which although not time-limited, would cause problems of dereliction if the use were abandoned. Such developments would include those having significant environmental effects, and also those likely to occur on greenfield, and/or rural locations, such as holiday villages/theme parks, petrol stations, and incinerators.

7 Planning guidance should be issued to encourage this approach, to include examples of model conditions, and emphasise the importance of subsequent enforcement. Cross references would need to be made as to how the six tests in Circular 1/85 would need to be applied to justify such conditions.

8 The Department of Trade and Industry should be encouraged to adopt the same line in negotiating consents for power station buildings.

9 Consideration should be given to amending the GDO, such that operators with permitted development powers to erect specialist structures which are incapable of being reused and are unsightly and potentially dangerous if left abandoned, should consult with local planning authorities on rehabilitation proposals before the use is likely to cease. This could be applicable to gas holders; settling tanks on water and sewage works sites. There is already a provision in the GDO in relation to the removal of satellite dishes when they are no longer needed (Class H, Part 1).

Rehabilitation Conditions with Financial Guarantees

10 Any ideas of a more formal system of financial guarantees should be kept under review until experience has been gained on the frequency and seriousness of financial failure or default on rehabilitation conditions for built development.

11 Any planning guidance that is issued on the subject of rehabilitation conditions should also clarify the circumstances within which financial guarantees are already being used and the financial provisions that have been found to be the most effective.

Extending Local Authority Powers

12 The Regulations for which provision has already been made in connection with existing S.215 powers, should be introduced in order that any expenditure incurred by a local authority which has not been recovered

from the operator, could be put as a charge on the land.

13   A new provision should be introduced into the Act similar to S.215 but to carry out rehabilitation works allowing entry onto private land deemed derelict.

14   This new provision should allow the cost of the rehabilitation works to be charged back to the landowner and placed as a charge on the land.

Tax Relief on Rehabilitation Expenditure

15   Consideration should be given to introducing legislation to allow carry-back provisions on rehabilitation expenditure incurred within three years after the cessation of trade.

Tax on the Holding of Derelict Land

16   Further detailed research should be undertaken on the practicalities and impact of implementing a tax on the holding of derelict land, before considering it as a long term possibility.

Timescales for Implementation

25   A higher profile should be given to the concept of rehabilitation through the use of the existing planning system to run alongside environmental protection powers. Legislative changes to provide more focused powers to prevent future dereliction should be introduced gradually. Recommendations on short, medium and long term actions for implementing policy changes are summarised in the main report. Any changes would need to be subjected to prior consultation with affected parties, and when implemented, be accompanied by clear guidance on the use of new powers.

CHAPTER ONE

Introduction

Preventing Derelict Land: Research Objectives

1.1 The Government is committed to the reclamation and re-use of vacant and derelict land. Reclaiming sites can contribute towards a reduction in the pressure for development on greenfield sites by providing sites for new development as well as achieving an improvement in the environment. This commitment fits within the concepts of sustainable development namely to minimise the use of scarce land resources for development and to maximise the efficiency with which previously developed land is recycled.

1.2 The Environment White Paper *This Common Inheritance* states that on the basis of the 'polluter pays principle', the costs of dealing with contamination and dereliction should be placed on those responsible for causing the damage. In 1988 the National Audit Office report on Derelict Land Grant (DLG) questioned the use of public expenditure in reclaiming land made derelict by private sector owners and operators. The consequence of adopting the polluter pays approach to site reclamation for built development would be to shift the burden of leaving the site in a state capable of reuse onto the landowner or occupier. This in turn would reduce the call on public funds to cover the cost of site 'restoration' and reduce the flow of additional land into dereliction. This is likely to be perceived as a significant shift in the existing principles of development rights, but is fundamental to considering any new provisions to prevent dereliction through the development process.

1.3 In line with this thinking, the Government produced a Consultation Paper *Proposals to Prevent Land Becoming Derelict*, in February 1992 which put forward two options to help deal with this situation. These were:

- the use of restoration conditions on planning permissions for new developments; and

- an extension of local authority powers under S.215 to require owners and occupiers of derelict land to undertake its reclamation.

1.4 Responses to the Consultation Paper indicated widespread support from local authority associations, individual authorities, environmental organisations and interest groups for the overall concept of preventing future dereliction. Support amongst industrial associations and individual companies was somewhat less, but not dismissive. Many respondents recognised that the two options could be complementary. However, they also raised a range of practical issues which needed to be addressed if either was to be successfully introduced and effective in its implementation.

1.5   The purpose of the current research has been to follow up the Government's consultation exercise and to examine whether the planning system might be used to prevent non-mineral sites from becoming derelict in the future (see the research specification at Appendix A). Through interviews with interested parties, key actors in the development process and individual case studies, the research aims have been to:

- assess the effectiveness of the various options for using the planning system to ensure that reclamation takes place, and the costs that they would impose upon industry;

- advise the Department on how any such options might be implemented.

1.6   The issues that have been investigated are largely forward looking, namely the mechanisms that might be used in relation to current development proposals to prevent land from becoming derelict when those uses cease in the future. Such mechanisms are largely those that can be delivered by the planning system, particularly through the development control process. Associated fiscal measures that might be used are also considered. However, the starting point for any mechanism to be effective should be to promote an approach which will help change the climate of opinion about the use of land following the closure of an operation, and which will help landowners, operators and occupiers to be more aware of their stewardship role.

Study Approach

1.7   The study has been undertaken in four main stages between July 1994 and January 1995.

1.8   **Stage 1** sought to refine the options following a review of responses to the Department's Consultation Paper. A summary of responses to the Consultation Paper is given in Appendix B. From this, a checklist of issues to be addressed and possible obstacles to implementation were defined. A comparison of mechanisms used to tackle problems of dereliction overseas was also undertaken using professional contacts in the relevant countries and examining relevant literature sources.

1.9   **Stage 2** involved discussing the implications of the various means of preventing future dereliction with a range of interested parties in the planning and development fields. Thirty four interviews were conducted with representatives of:

- four local authority associations

- seven local authorities

- two development corporations

- English Partnerships

- five professional bodies and amenity societies

- five industry associations

- five financial institutions

- five local authorities and development agencies in Scotland.

1.10   The full list of interviewees is given in Appendix C. Half of the parties interviewed had previously submitted comments on the Government Consultation Paper. A semi-structured format was used and the checklist of topics covered is given in Appendix D.

1.11   **Stage 3** involved undertaking 40 case studies to provide a more detailed understanding of the applicability of the various mechanisms to particular sets of circumstances (including types of development and location). The case studies were divided between three groups involving:

(i)   existing mechanisms to prevent dereliction

(ii)   recent development without such provisions

(iii)   older development giving rise to derelict or recently reclaimed land.

1.12   The emphasis of the case study work within each of these groups varied but in each case involved discussions with the local planning authority, investigating the planning history of the site, and interviewing the developer, operator or occupier where they could be identified; this was not always possible in relation to the older developments.

1.13   The choice of case studies was made to give coverage to a range of:

- development types

- geographic areas

- mechanisms used.

1.14   Further details of the selection process is given in Appendix E, and the checklist of topics raised in the interviews for each group of case studies is given in Appendix F. The main points arising from each individual case study are described in Appendix G.

1.15   Finally, **Stage 4** involved evaluating the advantages and disadvantages of the pre-defined options against a set of evaluation criteria. These criteria were agreed with the Steering Group and were used systematically to describe the likely effects of introducing any of the options. Due to the wide ranging and complex nature of the subject matter, this evaluation is a largely qualitative rather than quantitative assessment.

Structure of this Report

1.16   Chapter 2 outlines the overall background to the study. It examines factors leading to dereliction and describes the current scale and nature of the problem. It also identifies the wider context in which any mechanisms to prevent land from becoming derelict would operate. This includes the dynamics of the development process and the way in which the planning system can, in general terms, influence the future use and/or condition of sites. The effects of other complementary mechanisms/legislation, including environmental legislation and financial measures such as the tax system, are considered. The essential features of the legal framework within which any future mechanisms would operate are also examined.

1.17   Chapter 3 sets out the options considered in this study for preventing land from becoming derelict. These include the two suggestions put forward in the 1992 Consultation Paper, together with other possibilities for extending local authority powers, and a range of financial measures. A resumé of any experience in the current use of these provisions as revealed by the case study work is given for each option, together with a discussion of the range of issues that would need to be tackled to make each into a workable proposition.

1.18   The systematic evaluation of each of these options against a common set of criteria is given in Chapter 4. This is based on professional judgement informed by opinions put forward by the organisations interviewed at Stage 2 and the case study work undertaken. The results of the evaluation are summarised in a comparative table giving the main implications of each of the options.

1.19   Chapter 5 gives our conclusions on the need for a change in attitude and in responsibilities for site reinstatement. The limitations of existing planning powers are summarised together with the factors that need to be considered in contemplating any changes to the planning system. The report ends with our recommendations for additional measures that should be considered as amendments to planning legislation and/or through the tax system to contribute towards preventing future dereliction, as well as to assist the problems of inherited dereliction.

CHAPTER TWO

Derelict Land and the Development Process

Introduction

2.1 Under the former derelict land grant (DLG) programme, around £100 million per annum was being provided to reclaim derelict sites in England. The equivalent sum under the reclamation programme within English Partnership's Investment Fund is currently about £115 per annum. The Welsh Development Agency is currently spending around £30 m a year on land reclamation. The equivalent Scottish programme is termed Local Enterprise Grant and for urban projects is administered by Scottish Enterprise.

2.2 Despite this investment, the pace of reclamation is only marginally in excess of the flow of additional sites into dereliction. According to the 1993 Derelict land Survey the stock of derelict land, in England some 40,000 ha in 1993, has only been marginally reduced through reclamation between 1988–1993. Thus whilst around 8,300 ha has been reclaimed, the flow of new land into dereliction has been some 7,400 ha. In Wales the stock of derelict land is estimated to be 8,000 ha in 1993, which represents a reduction of some 3,000 ha since 1988. In Scotland the stock of derelict land was 9,522 ha in 1993, compared with 8,297 ha in 1990.

2.3 This section of the report outlines the context for consideration of options to prevent land becoming derelict. It examines, in general terms, the main forces at play in the development process and how these influence the use and condition of sites. The role of the current planning system and the relevance of other provisions to control the condition of a site are also examined.

Derelict Land and The Development Process

2.4 In order to be able to implement and enforce any provisions to prevent land from becoming derelict, it is necessary to have a clear understanding of what constitutes 'derelict' land and the reasons for land becoming derelict.

2.5 At present there is no statutory definition of dereliction or derelict land. For the purposes of funding under the 'old' derelict land grant (DLG) system, it was regarded as 'land so damaged by industrial or other development that it is incapable of beneficial use without treatment'. This included buildings which had become so dilapidated that they were structurally unsound. Using this definition, land is derelict where some form of reclamation works are necessary to bring the site back into a condition such that it is capable of development or other use without 'extra over' costs. The definition of derelict land as a 'trigger' for action and rehabilitation standards is considered in more detail in Section 3 of this report.

2.6   In simple terms, dereliction arises from the 'failure' of the development process in the recycling of developed sites because development costs exceed the potential value of the completed development. The economics of the property development process can be summarised as follows:

development cost < value = (re)development

development cost > value = no development.

2.7   In order to minimise costs and maximise value, by limiting site constraints and reducing as much as possible on-going liabilities and risk, a greenfield site will (all other things being equal) be more attractive than one already developed.

2.8   In practice the property development equation is much more complex. For example, a range of external and site specific factors will influence the timing and prospect of a site being redeveloped rather than becoming derelict. Factors will include:

- on-site development costs (land, site preparation, construction, finance, fees and a margin for profit) which may take into account extra items such as decontamination or underground structures. A contribution to these costs may be made from external (public sector) sources such as English Partnerships (EP) 'gap funding';

- off-site infrastructure costs associated with opening up a site for development;

- development value (realised on disposal or as a capitalised rental stream) which may be 'supported' by rental guarantees from EP; and

- planning policies and economic development programmes which influence the investment decisions of potential developers including location, greenfield : brownfield site development and timing.

2.9   The **speed** with which land is recycled is also a product of national and local conditions. These include the state of the local and national economy (including interest rates), the local land market and the demand for and supply of alternative sites. Site specific characteristics such as location, existing use/value, development potential and planning policy context will also influence the timing of events. A particular difficulty exists in areas of low demand where the development costs of brownfield sites are high. In these circumstances, intervention in the land market by external (public) agencies may be necessary to bring about development. For example, direct policy initiatives (such as Enterprise Zones) may facilitate the redevelopment of sites which are, or might otherwise become, derelict.

2.10   Another complicating factor is the differing interests of players in the property development process. The time horizons for development, return on investment and risk exposure will vary between the owner/ occupier, developer/trader and investment fund. Each will have an influence on the timing and likelihood of an existing site being redeveloped.

2.11   There are several reasons why land may legitimately be held **vacant**, or become available and remain undeveloped. For example:

- land may be held as a 'non-productive' asset/resource for accounting purposes or to capitalise on future growth in land values/rental levels;

- land may be held for the future expansion of industry or operations.

2.12   It is likely that in these circumstances, of land being held as a resource, the owner would seek to prevent the land becoming derelict, thereby avoiding the additional costs in bringing the site back into productive use when the need arose. However, such land may become derelict over time.

2.13   On the other hand land may fall into a **derelict** state due to:

- the financial failure of the site owner/occupier leading to the 'abandonment' of the site;

- tax burdens (or incentives) leading to a site's neglect; and

- the piecemeal acquisition of land for comprehensive redevelopment (or new proposals such as major infrastructure projects) having a blighting effect.

The Nature of the Problem to be Tackled

Inherited Dereliction

2.14　Dereliction is not specific to a particular location, business sector or period of time and, as outlined in 2.2 above, the reasons for sites becoming derelict are numerous. However, the impact of structural change within the economy over recent years has had a significant impact on the total area of land becoming derelict. Research into the use by local authorities of derelict land grant (DLG) to reclaim sites for hard end use development *(Assessment of the Effectiveness of Derelict Land Grant in Reclaiming Land for Development, HMSO 1994)* has revealed that of all sites reclaimed during the period 1983–1990, almost 60% were in some form of industrial/ commercial use prior to reclamation. Almost a half of all sites reclaimed had become derelict five years or less prior to the first DLG application and almost two-thirds had become derelict less than 10 years before the DLG application.

2.15　These figures, together with site specific evidence from this study, indicate that the current scale and nature of derelict land is to a large extent the legacy of earlier industrial activities and structural change in the economy. Sites were often developed and used in an unregulated way. In many cases, the redundant structures and associated ground conditions left after the cessation of the use impose a particularly high cost on making the site capable of accommodating alternative development.

2.16　This is of relevance to the current study for two reasons:

(i)　there is a stock of older sites which may become derelict in the future unless some form of provision is made to tackle land now developed from becoming derelict;

(ii)　the nature of dereliction may change as the stock of older buildings is replaced either through the normal development process or with some form of public sector assistance, and as measures to control other aspects of site development and use take effect.

2.17　If the planning system, together with other complementary systems, is to be effective in tackling dereliction then appropriate measures need to be in place which can tackle both the underlying stock of derelict land and the continuing flow of sites into dereliction. This study is primarily focused on the second of these elements, measures to prevent land becoming derelict in the future.

2.18　Internal Arup research following the 1993 Derelict Land Survey suggests that of the total stock of derelict land, some 40% is contaminated. Whilst contamination is not the only reason for the sites being derelict it will account for part of the site preparation costs which are contributing to it remaining undeveloped. The provisions of the Environmental Protection Act 1990 should greatly reduce the risk of ground contamination from any new development. This is therefore of importance with regard to the prevention of dereliction.

Risk of Future Dereliction

2.19　Certain types of development are unlikely to pose a significant risk of future dereliction. In particular, residential properties (and new industrial and office accommodation) are likely to be recycled through normal market processes because the structures involved can be removed at a low net cost or be readily adapted to alternative use.

2.20　Whilst a large number of building types are capable of refurbishment and reuse for alternative purposes, the costs of conversion for some specialised types such as mill buildings or power stations can be high and may be unjustified by the value of the resultant building. Others are incapable of alternative use for structural, constructional or other reasons. Such developments could cover a wide range of privately owned uses including petro-chemicals, telecommunications, the water industry and the fast growing non-landfill industrial and medical waste disposal industry. Short life developments may also create a risk in the commercial environment for example in the retail sector where the extent of trading competition may lead to the possible abandonment of some superstores and out of town shopping complexes. Leisure facilities are also subject to changing consumer preferences and the all weather complexes and forest villages currently being developed could be amongst the derelict sites of the next century.

2.21 Besides the **nature of development**, the other factor that gives rise to a risk of future dereliction is its **location**. Sites in and around urban areas are more likely to be recycled through the normal workings of the property market than sites in the open countryside where planning policy constraints restrict acceptable alternative uses for sites. Hence there is a risk of future dereliction following closure of uses such as military establishments, prisons and hospitals in rural areas.

2.22 The incidence of dereliction from current mineral workings has virtually ceased because of the imposition and enforcement of restoration conditions on mineral extraction permissions, although past mining activities (spoil heaps, excavations and pits) still contribute around one third of all derelict land. Restoration conditions are also routinely applied to permissions for landfill sites. Restoration conditions have a particular meaning here in terms of Schedule 5 of the Town and Country Planning Act 1990, basically involving soil stripping and replacement. The concept of restoration as used in this report for non-mineral development equates to both site reinstatement and land being left in a condition such that it is capable of beneficial use without additional costs of site reclamation/preparation prior to redevelopment. The term rehabilitation is therefore used in preference.

2.23 Most planning permissions for non-mineral development do not include conditions or agreements relating to site reclamation or after-use. Central to this is the fact that the prevention of dereliction, per se, is not currently an explicit purpose of the planning system. Non-mineral development is assumed to be permanent, unless special reasons justify a temporary permission, and generally no specific consideration is given to the after-use of the site because of the long term/indefinite nature of the development. The future use and/or redevelopment of the site is not a material consideration in the determination of most planning applications. Future development of the site is, in effect, left to the normal workings of the property market and property development process.

The Role of the Planning System in Influencing the Future Use/Condition of Sites

2.24 The planning system is able to influence the present and future condition of sites through two principal mechanisms:

- placing 'obligations' on development as part of the development control process (through conditions or legal agreements attached to planning permission);

- default powers to require action to be taken (or through direct intervention) to rectify a particular situation arising from the action (or inaction) of a site owner/occupier. These default powers may be triggered by public health, safety or amenity considerations, or failure to comply with conditions.

2.25 A third area of intervention is through powers of compulsory purchase to take control of land. This may be used in association with other provisions.

2.26 Mechanisms aimed at influencing the nature of development such as **conditions** involve 'intervention' at the pre-development stage of the process. They are proactive, seeking to control future events and may be both positive (eg requiring the provision of a particular facility) or negative (eg not allowing a particular event to occur until such time as some other action has taken place; a 'Grampian' condition). Local authorities can take enforcement action against non-compliance with planning conditions. The requirements associated with conditions are transferred with changes in ownership.

2.27 Conditions may be reinforced by a **legal agreement** regulating development or the use of land. Under S.106 of the 1990 Planning Act (as amended) voluntary agreements can be made between the site owner and local authority which are enforceable against successors in title. Provision is made for a local authority to enter the land and carry out the operations and recover any expenses reasonably incurred from the person against whom the obligation is enforceable if there is a breach of a requirement in the planning obligation.

2.28 **Default powers** (such as under S.215 of 1990 Planning Act) by contrast respond to events when issues of amenity are threatened and may require steps to be taken by the owner/occupier of a site to remedy the situation. They largely relate to the activity or site condition in existence at a particular point in time and as such they are reactive.

2.29   Thus, whereas the imposition of conditions and negotiation of a planning obligation are associated with the granting of permission in advance of development, default powers are by their very nature provisions which can only be invoked against existing buildings and activity.

2.30   Comparable actions under other legislation include:

- *Repairs Notices* (S.48 Planning (Listed Buildings and Conservation Areas) Act 1990) to secure works to preserve a listed building from deteriorating or falling into disrepair. Under the provisions of the Act a local authority may compulsorily acquire a building in order to secure its preservation, although compensation is payable at the current market value unless the authority can demonstrate that the building has been deliberately allowed to fall into disrepair for the purposes of justifying its demolition and redevelopment.

- *Dangerous Structures Notices* (S.77 Building Act 1984) to secure works of repair or restoration or, should the owner elect, demolition of a building or structure which is dangerous. Under S.77 material from a demolished building must be cleared from the site. S.79 of the Act provides similar powers where a building or structure by virtue of its ruinous or dilapidated condition is seriously detrimental to the amenities of the area.

2.31   The extent to which these types of default powers could be transferred to the prevention of dereliction is limited, however, because each has a specific rationale:

- Listed building legislation provides authorities with the power to order work, carry out work itself or compulsorily acquire buildings for the purpose of securing their preservation. This is because of their value as buildings of architectural or historic interest, rather than to prevent the building from becoming derelict per se.

- Dangerous Structures Notices seek to secure the repair or removal of buildings not because they are derelict but because they are dangerous and pose a threat to public safety. Although most buildings which are the subject of a notice are also likely to be derelict, the condition of a building warranting action has to be severe and is unlikely to apply to a large number of derelict buildings.

2.32   A feature of each of these notices is that, unlike enforcement action, all are discharged after compliance with the terms of the notice. As a consequence, whilst their effect transfers with ownership, once the requirements have been complied with no further action is possible without further notices being issued.

2.33   In practice the extent to which local authorities can influence the use and condition of sites is constrained by the specific circumstances under which particular powers can be used and case law. It is also limited by the extent of permitted development rights granted under the General Development Order, and the jurisdiction of local authorities in determining applications for development, which excludes for example certain Crown development and consents under the Energy Act.

Other Mechanisms for Controlling the Condition of Sites

2.34   The **Environmental Protection Act 1990** and current Environment Bill formalise the 'polluter pays principle' to site ownership, use and development, in particular responsibility and liability for contamination. In that the risks of ground contamination from new development are thereby reduced, this environmental legislation is assisting the prevention of derelict land in the future.

2.35   In relation to sites already contaminated, the underlying principle is that the primary responsibility rests with the person who caused or knowingly permitted the contamination to occur. Under the provisions of the Environment Bill, enforcing authorities will have the power to undertake works and secure their uncovered costs by way of a charge on the land. The requirement for remedial action to achieve the control and treatment of sites such that they are 'suitable for use' aims to reduce damage from past activities and allow contaminated land to be kept in or returned to beneficial use wherever practicable.

2.36   **Waste management controls** (under Part II of the Environmental Protection Act 1990) include provision for 'Certificates of Completion' relating to the hand-over of landfill sites. These indicate compliance with regulations but do not provide a 'guarantee' as to site conditions following completion of operations.

2.37   Other informal mechanisms exist for controlling the condition of sites. Firstly some industry specific **codes of practice** include references to site rehabilitation. Already a number of larger minerals operators and associations such as the Silica and Moulding Sands Association have devised codes of practice which spell out preferable restoration methods. The British Wind Energy Association encourages its members to clear sites on decommissioning of windfarms and other association such as the Chemical Industries Association have highlighted codes of practice for their members. Industry association codes of practice can be used to demonstrate that a responsible attitude is being undertaken and to enhance the overall reputation of that industry.

2.38   Secondly, **Environmental Assessment** techniques have encouraged decommissioning or rehabilitating the land to be considered explicitly, particularly where the operational life of a development is expected to be limited. Although it is not mandatory, this encourages decommissioning to be thought about at project planning stage rather than left to the end of the operational process. Appropriate mitigation mesures can therefore be incorporated. Demonstration of environmental awareness is increasingly used as a marketing tool especially by larger industries dealing with unusual or potentially disruptive processes.

2.39   Thirdly, contractual agreements between the landowner and the operator/leaseholder can also make explicit provision for the eventual condition of a site. **Leasehold agreements** can include conditions requiring the lessee to return the site to the lessor in its original condition on expiry of the lease (see case study 2.13). This places an obligation on the former to undertake any work to make good any damage resulting from occupation of the site. This may be financed through a sinking fund for building repairs and maintenance. This illustrates that the principle of site rehabilitation is already established in some commercial investment decisions. Health and Safety Executive requirements may also ensure partial rehabilitation of sites for particular operations such as petrol stations (see case study 2.11).

Fiscal Influences on Preventing Dereliction

2.40   Financial mechanisms (largely tax-based) can be used to considerable effect to encourage or discourage certain activities. In principle, by imposing taxes on buildings, land or other assets, Government creates incentives by setting appropriate charges based on the relative costs of individual action.

Rating and Tax Charges

2.41   Widely used to modify behaviour in other areas, there are few fiscal measures which encourage the prevention or rehabilitation of derelict land. Indeed some measures may have had side effects that run counter to the objective of preventing land from becoming derelict. For example, a former rating system allowed an exemption from rates if a building was not fit for occupation. This led some landowners to remove the roofs from their vacant properties in order to minimise tax liability, but thereby making them unfit for occupation. This action also prevented their potential re-use at a later date. Although this loophole was closed in the mid 1980s, it illustrates the potential impact of property taxation on incentives to hold land in a state fit for an alternative use.

2.42   At present there is no fiscal penalty on holding land in a derelict state. For commercial properties, empty buildings are automatically charged at half the standard business rate. However, unoccupied property rates are not payable where the structures concerned are either classified as industrial (or are listed buildings). Furthermore, derelict sites may be assessed at zero value therefore negating any business rate charge. As such, landowners actually have no fiscal incentive to rehabilitate a derelict site to a vacant state as this could incur a demand for payment of business rates. Consequently, holding land in a vacant state (which does not impose any environmental or amenity costs on the locality) may be taxed, whereas holding land in a derelict state attracts no tax liability.

Tax Relief

2.43   The tax system can also be used to encourage actual rehabilitation or restoration activity. In the minerals extraction industry, operators can offset restoration expenditure against income to minimise their tax liability. This encourages mineral operators to undertake restoration even after the income from the site has ceased. For non-minerals development however, tax relief is not normally allowed for rehabilitation expenditure as it is not regarded as an operating expense.

2.44   There are therefore very limited fiscal incentives related to derelict land in this country. The current tax system does not discourage the holding of land in a derelict state and provides little tax incentive to undertake rehabilitation expenditure. Examples of fiscal measures used in other developed countries to encourage site rehabilitation and/or prevent dereliction are given in Section 3.7.

CHAPTER THREE

Options to Prevent Land from Becoming Derelict

Introduction

3.1   Five sets of measures have been considered in this study. Two of these equate with the options put forward in the 1992 Consultation Paper, and relate specifically to aspects of the planning system. A third option combines financial measures with a planning control. The remaining two options are financial measures, which might be used in general support of planning objectives.

3.2   Before describing the mechanics of each of the options there are two sets of definitions that would be required in order to turn the concepts behind derelict land prevention into workable propositions: a definition of dereliction, including triggers to initiate action, and standards of site rehabilitation.

Definitions of Dereliction

3.3   In order to prevent dereliction, it is important to foresee and seek to control the sets of circumstances that may give rise to this state. Three different types of development can be envisaged, each necessitating a different approach to the prevention of dereliction, although in each case the operation of the land market and/or other forces may bring about redevelopment and prevent dereliction without intervention through the planning system.

3.4   Firstly, there are **temporary buildings or structures** which by their very nature have a limited lifespan, for example wind turbines. These developments have no practicable alternative use and may be in sensitive locations. In these circumstances the building or structure would become derelict at the end of its design life or on cessation of the operations, which ever was the sooner. Time limited planning permissions may therefore appropriately include a site reinstatement condition requiring removal of structures and return of the site to its former state. Action to comply with the condition and prevent dereliction would be triggered by (or at a specified period after) the cessation of a use.

3.5   Secondly, there may be particular **industrial activities involving specialist structures** where it can be reasonably established from the outset that there are no practicable alternative uses of the site and where decommissioning/site clearance costs will be high, for example large scale chemical works. The site could potentially become derelict on cessation of the use because the site/buildings are incapable of alternative use without significant site reclamation costs. Appropriate action could be taken at the time of granting planning permission by way of a condition requiring the removal of the specialist structures if or when that use ceased. Site reinstatement could be to a brownfield state or to its former use depending on the circumstances. In practice it is likely to be to a brownfield state to allow redevelopment without incurring 'extra over' costs of site preparation.

3.6   The third category is other **'permanent' industrial development**. Such buildings are likely to be capable of being used for purposes other than that for which permission was originally granted. In these circumstances establishing when a building has become derelict is more difficult. The cessation of the use as a trigger for action is not appropriate and the reinstatement of the site by the removal of the building would be unreasonable.

3.7   The Environmental Protection Act uses physical thresholds relating to specified levels of contaminants to trigger remedial action. Using this analogy, it may be possible to define dereliction in relation to the physical condition of a building or site whereby particular characteristics would trigger action. In this respect, case law *(see Trustees of the Earl of Lichfield's Estate v Secretary of State for the Environment [1985] JPL 251)* has addressed the question of the state of a building (for the purposes of determining whether permitted development rights exist under the GDO) as a legitimate test under the existing planning system. This recognises the structural state of a building, and whether it is capable/incapable of use for its intended (approved) purpose, as a planning consideration. It is considered that the principles established in this case could be extended to the prevention of dereliction and the identification of a 'trigger' for action. Hence the prevention of dereliction would be achieved through the proper maintenance of buildings where the trigger for action would be defined in relation to the state of the site/building. The necessary action would be to maintain the building to prevent it from falling into a state of disrepair (ie dereliction) rather than demolish it and to return the site to its pre-development state.

3.8   In each case action to prevent dereliction might be undertaken voluntarily by the site owner in compliance with a condition, through enforcement action by the local authority against non-compliance with that condition, or as default action against the state of the site.

Rehabilitation Works and Standards

3.9   The scope of work involved in rehabilitating a site such that it can be used for other purposes needs to be defined. This begs the question of whether it is possible to define a minimum standard of rehabilitation based on the condition that the site should be left in, or whether it is better to define the works deemed necessary on a particular site.

3.10   Data collected during the study suggests that the cost of reclamation/rehabilitation works can vary widely as a percentage of development costs and as total amounts. Costs ranged from less than 0.5% of development costs (a windfarm) to an estimated 8% (holiday village). Costs will therefore vary depending on the nature of the development (eg above ground structures only and/or underground structures) but also the standard of rehabilitation expected on the site. As a consequence it is not practicable to suggest a common percentage figure be adopted for particular types of development.

3.11   Instead, defining rehabilitation objectives in terms of physical works and identifying particular features to be removed/provided, such as the removal of structures (and buildings) not suitable for alternative use and ensuring land stability, is a more practicable approach.

3.12   This could be used as the basis of a 'national minimum standard' of rehabilitation. It would then be possible for local authorities to negotiate within this national framework the actual and site-specific rehabilitation requirements to reflect local circumstances. This could provide a degree of certainty about future physical and financial commitments and would avoid the significant uncertainty which may result from a condition requiring that the developer and local authority discuss these matters some time before the use ceases on site.

3.13   A refinement of the 'national minimum standard' approach is to adopt the principle that any works to a site to prevent it from becoming derelict would allow a **similar alternative use** to be developed on the site without additional site preparation costs. Thus any structures on, over, or under ground would have to be removed and the site made stable. Adopting the principle of 'suitable for use', rehabilitation would be to a standard appropriate for a comparable alternative use occupying the site rather than a higher standard to allow the site to be developed for more 'sensitive' uses. These additional costs would be borne by the incoming developer. Thus if an industrial site was or was likely to become derelict, the obligation would be on the site owner to remove all structures to allow a similar use onto the site. Issues of ground contamination, it is assumed, would be dealt with by controls under the EPA. Should another developer wish to redevelop the site for housing then any additional requirements in terms of site preparation would be borne by them. In this way a balance would be struck between the costs associated with obligations of the site owner and the aspirations of the site developer.

3.14 The difficulty with any standard of rehabilitation is that it is established at the time of granting permission for development for an eventuality which, if it occurs at all, is likely to take place a number of years later. In order to provide a degree of certainty the rehabilitation standard should not change to reflect different/enhanced expectations of site rehabilitation in the future. However, this would have the effect of limiting future standards of rehabilitation to the expectations and technology available today.

Rehabilitation Conditions

3.15 The imposition of restoration conditions on planning permissions is already widely employed in the control of mineral extraction. Site restoration achieves the replacement of soils and together with appropriate aftercare allows for a positive after-use such as agriculture, forestry or nature conservation. The idea of this first option is therefore to extend this provision to relevant categories of non-mineral development to seek to rehabilitate sites so that they can be easily used by others. The categories of development at risk of future dereliction are described in Section 2.3 and those most suitable for the application of rehabilitation conditions are summarised at the end of this section.

3.16 This option is most directly related to the 'polluter pays principle' and would seek to ensure that after cessation of a particular activity an alternative use could locate on the site without incurring additional site preparation costs associated with clearing the site of derelict structures. Such conditions would thus have the effect of placing an obligation on the applicant to reinstate the site. These conditions would be transferred with the land as a duty on the existing or any subsequent owner.

Lessons from the Mineral Extraction Industry

3.17 The reason why non-mineral developments have not been more widely subject to rehabilitation conditions is that such developments have been regarded as permanent. The exception is time-limited permissions where permission is granted because the development, by its nature, is temporary. Temporary permissions should not be granted on the grounds of amenity. In addition, unlike minerals development which is essentially a destructive process, most other forms of development have the potential to improve land or increase its value.

3.18 A finite mineral resource means that there is a fixed time horizon to work towards, albeit in the case of some hard rock quarries this may be 60+ years. Permissions are therefore time limited and provision is frequently made for progressive restoration throughout the life of a mineral working. The type of after-use or state in which the site should be left and the timing of restoration can be established from the outset. As a result, restoration conditions can be specific in their requirements.

3.19 In addition, as a large proportion of minerals development takes place in rural locations where other types of development would be unacceptable on policy grounds, sites are often restored to their previous use, generally agriculture. For non-minerals development, however, rehabilitating sites to their previous use would not necessarily be desirable. Given the uncertainty concerning future uses on a site the principle of 'suitable for use', discussed in Section 3.1 above, is considered an appropriate basis for establishing a standard of rehabilitation.

3.20 Conditions currently used in minerals development to ensure other site resources are not lost (such as methods of soil stripping or storage of topsoils and subsoils which enable restoration to be largely a self-contained process) would also be difficult to apply to non-mineral development. With no definite end use or time horizon in mind, these resources may not be used and the obligation to rehabilitate the site may not in any case require their reuse if another type of built development were to replace that covered by the condition.

Compatibility with Circular 1/85 Tests

3.21 S.70 of the Town and Country Planning Act 1990 enables local authorities to grant planning permission 'subject to such conditions as they think fit'. This does not mean 'as they please' and Circular 1/85 ('The

Use of Conditions in Planning Permissions') identifies six tests for a condition to be valid. These are that conditions are:

- necessary
- relevant to planning
- relevant to the development to be permitted
- enforceable
- precise; and
- reasonable in all other aspects.

3.22 A number of interviewees were of the view that conditions requiring rehabilitation for non-mineral development would have difficulty meeting the six tests of Circular 1/85. An examination of the compatibility of rehabilitation conditions for built development reveals the difficulties involved in transferring the principles established in the mineral extraction industry to other development. This is demonstrated as follows:

- *Necessity*: this requires that local authorities ask whether planning permission would have to be refused if that condition were not imposed. The Circular makes clear that the argument that a condition will do no harm is no justification for its imposition. A condition ought not to be imposed unless there is a definite need for it. In the case of permanent development where often the land can readily be recycled for other uses, it is doubtful that a rehabilitation condition could be so material as to make development unacceptable without it. This is because the condition would be being imposed for a situation that may never occur.

  For certain types of development however, such as those involving highly customised structures in sensitive locations such as wind turbines and certain forms of communication masts, it may be that without such conditions, permission would need to be refused.

- *Relevance to Planning*: at the present time, the prevention of dereliction is not, per se, an explicit planning policy objective. The interpretation of planning law is ultimately a matter for the Courts, but there may be scope for advising on the circumstances where the prevention of dereliction may be a material planning consideration.

- *Relevant to the Development to be Permitted:* Circular 1/85 makes clear that it is not sufficient that a condition is related to planning objectives; it must also be called for by the nature of the development permitted or its effects on the surroundings. As with the first test, this test could only apply if the need to remove the development at some later date is material to the decision. This is only likely to be the case for specific types of development.

- *Enforceable:* precision in the wording of conditions will be crucial for effective enforcement. In practical terms this is likely to be one of the more difficult tests to meet if rehabilitation conditions were applied to permanent development. Of central importance would be an agreed definition of 'derelict' to trigger action. Clear guidance from the DOE would be required to assist local authorities with the practical difficulties of wording conditions including advice similar to that in Appendix B of Circular 1/85 regarding conditions which are unacceptable.

- *Precise:* Circular 1/85 makes clear that conditions requiring specific works to be carried out should state what these works are and when this must be done. This may be difficult for permanent development where the timing of works may be unknown, but could be triggered by the condition of the building.

- *Reasonable:* this relates to the first test of necessity and like this, is linked to the specific nature and detail of the development.

  From this review of the tests set out in Circular 1/85 it is apparent that, at best rehabilitation conditions may, in the first instance, need to be limited to a specific range of developments. It is likely that the philosophy and emphasis of Circular 1/85 will need to be restated so that the prevention of dereliction becomes a legitimate objective of the planning process.

Ability to Review Conditions

3.23 S.73 of the Town and Country Planning Act 1990 makes provision for conditions to be removed or varied. This allows for reconsideration of the purpose of a condition (but not the principle of development) at any time after it has been imposed. This could accommodate those circumstances where a condition, requiring removal of a structure after a specified period of time, needs to be reconsidered in the light of the prevailing circumstances (eg the building merited listing). Equally, a time-limited permission could be reconsidered in advance of its expiry. However, the uncertainty created by future permissions being withheld or new conditions being placed on subsequent applications is a concern of the development sector, particularly as the procedures can be time consuming, costly and offer no guarantee of success.

3.24   In theory the details of a rehabilitation scheme could be decided nearer the time that it was required. However, this is unlikely to be acceptable to the development sector as it would result in greater uncertainty about the future liabilities and costs. In addition, applicants would lose their right of appeal after six months of their permission. Even the scope to amend a condition under S.73 was considered too uncertain in these circumstances.

Form of Rehabilitation Conditions to be Evaluated

3.25   The concept to be taken forward for evaluation is that rehabilitation conditions requiring site reinstatement could be more widely used for at least three categories of development in order to prevent future dereliction. These relate to developments which are:

(i)   temporary (the development has a limited life span and the desired end state is known when permission is granted);

(ii)   specialised (the structures are unlikely to be reusable for an alternative purpose);

(iii)   located in sensitive areas where permission would not have been granted except for that particular use.

3.26   In addition there may also be other types of industrial development when a condition to ensure the proper maintenance of buildings may be appropriate.

3.27   Examples were found in the case study work of rehabilitation conditions being successfully negotiated with developers for all three categories of development listed above. Often these categories may be overlapping. The two windfarm developments (case study nos. 1.01 and 1.10) and the transmission mast (case study no. 1.06) fell into all three categories. The chalet development (case study no. 1.02) was in the third category.

3.28   The wording of such conditions as illustrated by the case study examples is shown in Boxes 1–3.

Box 1:   Rehabilitation Conditions for 15 Year Permission for Windfarm in an Area of Special Landscape

"... All development above ground level shall be removed and the moorland soil reinstated within 12 months of the cessation of electricity generation from the site or 30th June 2010 AD whichever is the sooner.

(i)   Each wind turbine generator shall be maintained in a good state of repair so as to be capable of continuous operation in appropriate wind conditions.

(ii)   Unless otherwise agreed with the Local Planning Authority, any wind turbine generator which remains out of normal operation for a period exceeding 12 months shall be dismantled and removed from site immediately".

(see case study no. 1.10).

Box 2:   Rehabilitation Condition for Five Year Permission for Telecommunication Mast in a National Park

"On or before that date, the mast shall be permanently removed from the land and the site shall be reinstated to its former condition unless an application to extend the permission has been approved in writing ..."

(see case study no. 1.06)

3.29   With the benefit of hindsight, the authority now feel, however, that wording of the condition shown in Box 2 could have been improved. No specific standard of restoration was set other than to remove and restore. Although damage to the site is likely to be minimal, the authority feel they could have clarified exactly what needed to be removed from the site (for example, underground servicing) to avoid difficulty at a later date.

3.30   The only case found where a rehabilitation/restoration condition had been imposed on a permanent development was on a chalet development (case study 1.02). Here the permission would not normally have been granted, given the sensitivity of the location in historic terms and its remoteness. However, a study of tourism potential commissioned by the local authority had specifically identified this area as an area of growth where such development should be welcomed.

Box 3:   Rehabilitation Condition for Chalet Development in a Rural Area

"In the event of the chalet site ceasing to operate, all chalets and any building erected within the site, shall be removed/demolished and the land reinstated to its former use to the satisfaction of the local planning authority".

(see case study no. 1.02)

3.31   The authority concerned acknowledges that the lack of precision in the wording of the condition shown in Box 3 is a potential problem for future enforcement, together with the fact that the chalets have now been leased to private individuals causing fragmentation of ownership.

3.32   The form of condition seeking reinstatement of a site once a time-limited operation has ceased to be evaluated in Section 4.2 of this report is shown in Box 4.

Box 4:   Illustrative Model Form of Rehabilitation Condition for Site Reinstatement Following a Temporary Operation

This permission is for a limited period of 15 years.

Within 12 months of the final cessation of operations on any relevant part of the site under this permission, or the final cessation of uses in a building hereby permitted on any relevant part of the site, that part of the site shall be cleared of buildings/structures on, in, under or over land, levelled, covered with topsoil and seeded with grass.

(If appropriate the condition could be extended to read: 'or such other scheme of reinstatement submitted to and agreed in writing by the Local Planning Authority').

3.33   The form of condition seeking site reinstatement if/when specialised structures are no longer required for their original use to be evaluated in Section 4.2 is shown in Box 5.

Box 5:   Illustrative Model Form of Rehabilitation Condition for Site Reinstatement for Specialised Structures

Within 12 months of the final cessation of operations on any relevant part of the site under this permission, or the final cessation of uses in a building hereby permitted on any relevant part of the site, that part of the site shall be cleared of buildings/structures on, in, under or over land and levelled.

(If appropriate the condition could also specify that the site should be covered with topsoil and seeded with grass. The condition could also be extended to read: 'or such other scheme of reinstatement submitted to and agreed in writing by the Local Planning Authority').

3.34   In addition, a condition requiring the proper maintenance of buildings may be appropriate for other forms of permanent development. This would require a more fundamental shift in thinking and would require further consideration of the particular types of circumstances where there was a risk of dereliction. This concept is not taken further in this report but an illustrative form of condition is given in Box 6 to engender further interest.

Box 6: Illustrative Model Form of Rehabilitation Condition Requiring the Proper Maintenance of Buildings

This permission shall enure for the benefit of the land unless or until the development is incapable of (beneficial) use for the purposes for which permission was granted, or such alternative use as may have been permitted by virtue of S.70 of the Town and Country Planning Act 1990 or the provisions of the Town and Country Planning (General Development) Order 1988.

At such time as the development is incapable of use the site shall be rehabilitated in accordance with a scheme to be agreed with the Local Planning Authority.

(If appropriate, the condition could specify that: 'all buildings and structures, together with such other development permitted as part of any subsequent planning permission (or under the provisions of the GDO) on, in, under or over land shall be removed from the site').

Financial Guarantees

3.35   Financial guarantees could be used to reinforce rehabilitation conditions for the purposes of preventing dereliction. These would be attached to the rehabilitation conditions at the time that planning permission was granted. In effect, the financial guarantee would relate to the anticipated cost of undertaking the works specified by the rehabilitation condition. Financial guarantees therefore represent an advance on the liability that the operator has accepted in agreeing to a rehabilitation condition. If the operator completes the rehabilitation works then the financial guarantee would be returned. However, in the event of default, the financial guarantee would revert to the local authority to cover the outstanding rehabilitation cost.

Determining the Amount of the Financial Guarantee

3.36   In order to prevent dereliction the amount of the financial guarantee required from the developer should equal the eventual cost of rehabilitation. This would ensure that the full rehabilitation cost could be financed from the financial guarantee should the operator default.

3.37   Assessing the future cost of rehabilitation after the present use has ceased is a complex area. As already discussed in relation to rehabilitation conditions, there is considerable uncertainty regarding when–if at all– rehabilitation would be required for built development. Furthermore, it is also difficult to determine exactly what site rehabilitation would be involved to return the site to the standard set in the rehabilitation condition.

3.38   Only one example was found in the case study work (no. 1.10) where a guarantee of £40,000 was sought to cover the removal of windfarm structures, index linked to the RPI. It is not known how precisely dismantling costs were estimated, but some uncertainty is implied by the fact that the same operator had a financial guarantee in place for a similar development in another part of the country for half this amount.

3.39   The costs of site clearance and reinstatement (including administration) for the chalet development (case study no. 1.02) were estimated by the local authority at £170,000.

3.40   Problems in assessing the eventual rehabilitation cost could be countered by arranging for a periodic review of the financial guarantee to ensure that it is still in line with a revised estimate of the costs. However, this would remove one of the advantages from the use of rehabilitation conditions which is that they provide a degree of certainty to the development industry. Periodically revising the sum of the financial guarantee would generate instability in the development process.

3.41   Furthermore from the perspective of preventing dereliction, the cost to the operator of defaulting on the financial guarantee would be central to his incentive to undertake site rehabilitation.

Cash-Based Deposits

3.42   Simple, cash-based deposit forms of financial guarantees would consist of an ex-ante payment of the full rehabilitation costs by the operator to the local authority. The local authority would hold the rehabilitation fund until such a time as the operator had discharged his rehabilitation liability–entitling him to a return of the funds–or had defaulted providing the local authority with the earmarked resources to undertake the rehabilitation works.

3.43   With a simple cash deposit form of financial guarantee, the relationship between the sum deposited as a financial guarantee and the actual cost of rehabilitation is central to the prevention of dereliction by the operator. Although the operator might still undertake site rehabilitation even if the actual costs outweigh the sum of the financial guarantee, this would be to maintain a good track record rather than the economic incentive effect of the financial guarantee. This illustrates that there are less quantifiable factors involved in making site rehabilitation decisions.

3.44   Cash-based financial guarantees involve the operator making an advance payment for a future liability. This has a direct implication in terms of development costs in that the eventual rehabilitation expenditure must be set aside before any income is generated from the operation of the site.

3.45   In order to lower these up front costs of financial guarantees, contributions to the financial guarantee could be made over a number of years. This would enable firms to spread the costs of providing the guarantee over the income operating phase of the development. Although this is generally more acceptable to developers, this method of building up a financial guarantee does not provide the local authority with the security of a full cash deposit before development commences. There remains a risk that the development may fail before the financial guarantee fund has been built up to a sufficient level to finance any site rehabilitation required. The likelihood of this occurring clearly depends on the timeframe over which the financial guarantee builds up.

Alternative Forms of Financial Guarantee–Bonds

3.46   Bank bonds relieve the operator of the up front cost of the financial guarantee which is replaced by an annual charge from the financial institution. This will be incorporated as an on-going expense.

3.47   Bank bonds consist of an agreement between the local authority the operator and a financial institution. In the event that the operator defaults on his rehabilitation condition, the financial institution will pay the sum of the bond to the local authority. The financial institution in turn will usually require a form of counter-indemnity from the operator. Furthermore the operator would expect to pay 2–3% of the bond amount per annum to the financial institution for acting as guarantor.

3.48   The limited experience of bonds required by the South Wales Local Acts for private opencast coal extraction is that they are provided by local banks. Typically ranging from £50,000 to £100,000, these involve charges of around 2–3% pa on the bond amount. However, bonds are available only for a fixed period which is usually limited to three years. This fixed period is determined on the basis of a commercial risk assessment of the operator and the guarantor. The use of financial guarantees to back restoration conditions in other sectors of the minerals extraction industry is very limited.

3.49   Severe doubts were expressed by interviewees from the financial services industry regarding the practicality of such bonding arrangements applied to built development.

3.50   The indefinite nature of built development and the lack of an established track record for each operator would complicate the commercial risk assessment necessary to issue a bond.

Alternative Forms of Financial Guarantee–Insurance

3.51   Another possible approach to lowering the initial costs of providing a financial guarantee is to use an insurance-based system. A straightforward arrangement would be where the third party insurer will pay the rehabilitation cost should the operator default. The insurer has no access to counter-indemnity and would require a premium from the operator based on a commercial risk assessment of the likelihood of default.

3.52 Common to all insurance systems is that there is an incentive for the operator to default on his rehabilitation condition. As the insurance company has no counter-indemnity, the operator would not face the full rehabilitation costs should he default. The premium absolves him of the incentive to rehabilitate his site. This would result in the rehabilitation costs being met by the insurance company. The implications of this are that the premiums for this insurance would rise. This would place a higher cost on firms especially those which have no track record or which have defaulted in the past.

3.53 A secondary issue related to insurance is that premium would be related to the likelihood of default at a particular moment. As such, premiums would tend to rise as the built development approached the end of its operational life. This could either bring forward the time when the operation is no longer viable–thereby creating dereliction–or result in insurance cover being withdrawn. Neither of these outcomes is desirable with regards to preventing dereliction.

3.54 The problem of perverse incentives–ie 'moral hazard'–and the implication for premiums means that insurance based tools as financial guarantees are unlikely to be operable in practice. Furthermore, commercial risk assessment would withdraw cover at the time that it is most needed. **This form of guarantee is not therefore carried forward for evaluation in Section 4.3.**

Alternative Forms of Financial Guarantee–Industry Funds

3.55 The use of industry funds has also been considered as a potential device for providing a financial guarantee for rehabilitation conditions on built development. For example, the Sand and Gravel Association restoration fund was established in 1974 to deal with the cost of restoring sites when member operators defaulted as a result of financial failure. It can only be called upon by the local authority if all necessary enforcement action has been taken, and there is no experience of its use to date.

3.56 The issues inherent in such a structure are that there are similar moral hazard incentives as in a regular insurance system due to the pooling of risk. This can be controlled if default results in exclusion from membership which then makes it more difficult for the operator to obtain planning permission in the future. Preliminary signals on the use of a landfill levy proposed in the Budget of November 1994 suggests that this might provide a fiscal incentive to join an industry-wide fund.

3.57 Built development generally does not classify into industry groups as readily as the minerals extraction or waste disposal industries. As there is no licensing system for most types of built development, there would be incentives implicit in such an approach to defaulting on rehabilitation conditions. There would be a danger of reputable operators having to fund disreputable operators, and high premiums being imposed on smaller and new enterprises. **This form of guarantee is not therefore carried forward for evaluation in Section 4.3.**

Triggering a Financial Guarantee

3.58 The effectiveness of financial guarantees also depends upon how easy it is to determine when a default of a rehabilitation condition has occurred. There are two possible situations:

- financial default;
- technical default.

3.59 In order to use the financial services industry to provide the tools for a financial guarantee, a definite trigger would have to be identified for the release of the financial guarantee. The financial services industry would not, on the whole, be prepared to undertake this policing and enforcement role.

3.60 An evaluation of the potential effectiveness of restoration bonds in the minerals industry conducted for the DOE Minerals Division in 1991 to 1993 *(Review of the Effectiveness of Restoration Conditions for Mineral Workings and the Need for Bonds)*, concluded that financial guarantees could theoretically deal with the issue of operator financial failure, because the trigger for release of funds would be clear cut. It would be much more difficult for bonds to be used to cover for technical default because of the scope for different interpretation of whether the necessary standard of restoration had been achieved. However, less than 5% of cases of non-compliance with restoration conditions were found to be due to financial failure of the operator, a proportion that remained unchanged from previous survey work in the mid 1970s. The DOE consulted on the study's recommendation that a wider use of restoration bonds was not justified.

3.61   In dealing with non-mineral development the same issues on triggers points would arise. In situations of financial default, the condition precipitating the release of the financial guarantee can be readily determined. In this context it is necessary only to ensure that the financial guarantee is held by another party and not regarded as part of the overall assets by the liquidator.

3.62   Conditions of technical failure would be more difficult to determine. These may involve some dispute between the operator and the local planning authority as to the requirements set out in the rehabilitation condition. An independent arbiter may need to be appointed to deal with such eventualities as occurred in the windfarm case study (no. 1.10). In any event, the costs of assessing whether a technical breach had occurred may be significant and would be borne by the individual parties.

Extending Local Authority Powers

Section 215 Powers

3.63   Existing powers under S.215 of the Town and Country Planning Act (1990) [equivalent to S.63–63A of the Town and Country Planning Act (Scotland) 1972] allow local planning authorities to enter land deemed to have a detrimental impact on amenity and undertake necessary remedial work.

3.64   Under S.215 of the Town and Country Planning Act where [it appears to the local planning authority that] the condition of land adversely effects the amenity of the area (or adjoining area), the local planning authority may serve a notice on the owner and occupier of land requiring steps to remedy the condition. The legislation is therefore aimed primarily at tidying up sites. If the specified steps are not been taken the local authority may enter onto the land to carry out the work and recover the costs from the landowner.

3.65   From the interviews conducted for this study it is apparent that S.215 Notices are regarded by local authorities as a rather protracted, cumbersome and ultimately 'toothless' provisions. The practical use of S.215 Notices (as currently drafted) is constrained by two principal considerations. These are being able to demonstrate that amenity has been adversely affected (and is not attributable to a lawful use or operation on the site) and, more significantly, being able to recover from the landowner the cost of works carried out in default, particularly where the landowner is not known or missing. In addition, timescales for action can be protracted.

Box 7:   Limitations of S.215 in Tidying Up Derelict Sites

Despite public pressure to act, the local authority did not feel it was in a position to enforce a S.215 notice in the case of a disused roadside cafe. The local authority deemed it likely that it would be challenged on the grounds that the condition of the site stemmed from an activity which was not in breach of planning control. The state of dilapidation and disamenity was therefore not sufficient to precipitate action under S.215.

(see case study no. 3.10)

3.66   There are three principal defences for a landowner to appeal against a S.215 Notice. These are that amenity is not adversely affected; the condition of the land is attributable to the carrying on of operations or use of land which is not a breach of planning control; the requirements of the notice are too onerous (or the period of compliance too short). Questions of amenity are difficult to assess and can lead to protracted negotiations both on the need for remedial action and the scope of works. The second of these is frequently used by landowners to justify the state of their site and is a cause of concern to local authorities.

3.67   The issue of the extent of works and their purpose, and the potential for 'dispute' between the LPA and recipient of a S.215 Notice is illustrated by comparison with works specified in a Repairs Notice. Whereas Repairs Notices in respect of listed buildings can require quite extensive works for the preservation of a building (and for which there is a clear purpose), the requirements of a S.215 Notice, on the grounds of amenity, are more difficult to justify. This was a particular shortcoming identified in Langbaurgh where a Repairs Notice was issued to help preserve a Grade II* listed walled garden (see case study no. 1.04).

3.68   One of the limitations of current legislation for recovering money from 'default works' is that although the Act includes provision for authorities to place a charge on the land (S.219), no Regulations have been made to bring this section into force. Even in cases where the private landowner will eventually bear the rehabilitation cost, the local authority must provide interim finance with the risk of not being able to recover the full restoration cost on completion.

3.69   In practice therefore S.215 Notices tend to be used for small scale tidying up of unsightly land (rather than large scale clearance works) where the landowner is likely to carry out the specified works or the costs are (relatively) small and are considered to be easily retrievable if the authority has to carry the works out in default.

Box 8:   Recovery of Costs for Works to Tidy Up a Leisure Site

In the case of Mullan Park, Chesterfield although the owner of the site could not be traced the local authority was able to recover its costs (including administrative costs) from another party with an interest in the land, in this case the mortgagee. By being able to trace the bank who held the title deeds for the site the local authority was able to obtain agreement that the costs of the works be met. However, the bank's willingness to comply with the requirements of the notice were likely to have been influenced by its desire to realise the value of the site over which they held a charge and where there was some (additional) value to be realised from a cleared site unfettered by any notices. It appears that the bank regarded the (relatively low) cost as reasonable for tidying up the site prior to sale. In cases where land is not registered this outcome would be more difficult to achieve and the timescales for action more protracted.

In this case S.215 powers coupled with a Dangerous Structures Notice were used to tackle the site conditions.

(see case study no. 1.05)

3.70   When the alternative powers with provision for default actioned by a local authority (S.215, Repairs Notice, Dangerous Structures Notice) are compared, the case study examples demonstrate that they are generally used in parallel rather than in isolation. This may be because one power achieves only a partial solution or that the provisions allow for 'default action' by the local authority only after site acquisition.

A New Provision

3.71   The extension of S.215 powers (to allow rehabilitation to proceed where the landowner was unknown or failing to take action) was put forward in the DOE Consultation Paper in 1992. A modified form of S.215 (or a new section of the Act) would enable local authorities to enter private land deemed derelict, rehabilitate the site and charge the cost of the rehabilitation back to the landowner.

3.72   Given the rationale for S.215 Notices (redressing harm to amenity arising from the use of a site rather than preventing land from becoming derelict) a separate section of the Act would be more appropriate than amendment to S.215. The specific provisions needed to make a new/amended section workable are discussed below.

3.73   A new S.215-type provision would, like the existing S.215, be a default power which could be used when a site becomes derelict. It would be reactive rather than proactive and its effect on preventing land from becoming derelict would be as a deterrent.

3.74   The grounds on which it would be possible for a local authority to take action would be specifically geared to dealing with sites which had become derelict. The provision would allow local authorities to undertake rehabilitation works where the landowner was unknown or failing to take action. It would be necessary for the local authority to demonstrate why the land was deemed to be derelict, and the nature of the rehabilitation works that should be carried out.

3.75   Under a new S.215 type provision there would need to be some right of appeal either to the Secretary of State or through the courts. The defences would be that the site was not derelict or that the requirements of the notice were too onerous (or the period of compliance too short). By definition, it would not be a defence, unlike the current S.215, that the state of the site was attributable to a lawful use or operation on the land (as dereliction is related to the lack of a beneficial use of the land in question).

3.76 In introducing a new provision it should be made explicit that it would cover site redevelopment difficulties resulting from underground structures as well as surface problems. The former often account for a large part of any site rehabilitation costs (but do not fall within the remit of existing S.215 powers).

3.77 Specific attention was given in the 1992 Consultation Paper to mechanisms for the recovery from the landowner of rehabilitation expenditure by local authorities and a range of options considered.

3.78 In some cases, rehabilitation costs may far outweigh the market value of a site, in spite of the increase in value due to site rehabilitation works. In these cases, recovery of rehabilitation expenditure may be significantly below 100% and local authorities will find it difficult to recover their outlay. Even if they were able to secure a charge over the land they would have to wait until the site is sold before achieving even a partial return.

3.79 For sites which cannot be 'profitably' rehabilitated, the value of the site at eventual transfer will always be less than the rehabilitation cost incurred. In such cases landowners are only likely to be encouraged to prevent land from becoming derelict if some form of penalties are associated with these proposals. This might include a penalty for non-compliance with the original notice as well as meeting the cost of the work. However the penalty may need to be set at a high level if rehabilitation costs are likely to far outweigh the value of the site.

Compulsory Purchase Orders

3.80 Local authorities play an important role in reclaiming some of the more difficult derelict sites. CPO powers are already used as part of this process. Indeed local authorities currently hold 16% of all derelict land (1994 Derelict Land Survey) and with other public bodies account for over a third of all derelict land.

3.81 As a mechanism for recovering rehabilitation expenditure, an extension of CPO powers may have some merit, subject to an efficient and equitable compensation scheme for landowners which does not provide incentives to leave land derelict in areas of low demand. However, local authorities are unlikely to have access to the necessary funds in order to make CPOs an effective mechanism for preventing dereliction.

3.82 CPOs can act as a 'stick' and 'carrot' to landowners to carry out rehabilitation work. The potential loss of title through CPO by a local authority (to recover the cost of rehabilitation carried out in default), may be a sufficient incentive for landowners to undertake private site rehabilitation rather than to hold the site as an asset in their books, perhaps over the real market value when rehabilitation costs are taken into account. As such CPO powers could provide an incentive to landowners to prevent dereliction.

3.83 However, there will still be those cases where the cost of rehabilitation will continue to outweigh the private net loss resulting from a CPO. As a result, local authorities would continue to accumulate high rehabilitation liabilities through their use of CPO powers. This implies an on-going deficit which can only be covered by public funds.

3.84 The complexity of the legal process associated with CPOs, together with the protracted timescales suggests that attention would need to be given to streamlining the process in some way if its use were to be extended. The majority of local authority interviewees in this study commented that CPOs are currently difficult to obtain and often not upheld by the Secretary of State.

3.85 The increased use of CPOs is not in line with the emphasis of English Partnerships on cooperation and agreement with the private sector. It is unlikely that sufficient funds would be made available to make them a serious deterrent to landowners in letting their land become derelict. **This option is not therefore considered further in the evaluation in Section 4.**

Tax Relief on Rehabilitation Expenditure

3.86   This section describes the option of using tax relief mechanisms to encourage the rehabilitation of derelict or worked out sites. Two tools are presented which would give the incentive to the existing landowner, with a further instrument which would provide an incentive to incoming developers to invest in derelict sites.

Carry-back Provisions

3.87   On-going rehabilitation expenditure is normally deductible against income as an operating expense in the year that it is incurred. However, tax relief is not normally available for rehabilitation expenditure that fails to meet revenue criteria. Expenditure treated as capital for tax purposes (as a result of case law decisions) does not attract tax relief as an operating expense. In addition, rehabilitation expenditure incurred after a site has ceased to be used would not normally obtain tax relief even if the work met revenue criteria for tax purposes.

3.88   In the minerals extraction industry there are carry-back provisions which encourage post-operation restoration. Under S.109 of the Capital Allowances Act (1990), minerals operators can offset restoration expenditure incurred within three years after cessation of trade against the trading income of the final accounting period. Although this does not offer support over a longer time frame, it does encourage substantial post-operations restoration to be undertaken.

3.89   Two changes would be required to existing tax legislation to bring the treatment of rehabilitation expenditure into line with the treatment of post-operations restoration in the minerals extraction industry. These are as follows:

(a)   The criteria which determine whether expenditure on existing property is eligible for tax relief would have to be widened to allow rehabilitation expenditure incurred either to prevent dereliction or to rehabilitate derelict sites to qualify.

(b)   Carry-back or set off provisions similar to, but possibly wider than, the S.109 provisions would have to be introduced. Such provisions could, for example, allow tax relief to be given to any company which is a member of a group, by relieving rehabilitation expenditure against the taxable profits of other members of the group.

Forward Provisions

3.90   To encourage operators to set aside funds for future rehabilitation expenditure, earmarked forward provisions could be included as a tax deductible expense. The tax credit would be obtained at the time the provision for qualifying rehabilitation expenditure is made rather then when the actual expenditure is incurred for qualifying rehabilitation expenditure. By allowing tax relief on such provisions, operators would have a tax incentive to build their rehabilitation budget at a time when their income stream is steady and positive.

3.91   Current tax legislation does not allow for forward provisions for the rehabilitation of built development to be tax deductible. It requires that tax relief can only be given on accepted operating expenses at the time the expense is actually incurred. Forward provisions do not meet the test of actually being expended and could, from the Inland Revenue's perspective, be used to minimise tax liability rather than to provide for rehabilitation.

3.92   As described in Section 3.7, some other countries do allow tax relief on forward provision in certain circumstances. Germany and Ireland are notable in allowing relief on forward provision, albeit within tightly controlled guidelines.

3.93   Nevertheless, if the provisions were made in the context of a financial guarantee secured by a third party, then there would be no utilisation of this rehabilitation fund as a tax minimisation strategy. By limiting the tax relief on rehabilitation expenditure to an agreed amount, efficient provisions would be made for rehabilitation. Rehabilitation would be implemented in line with the terms of the financial and legal agreement between the third party guarantor, the operator and the local planning authority.

3.94   The transfer of the title of a site which had a rehabilitation bond associated with it would need to include the transfer of the bond agreement to the purchaser and take into account tax relief obtained by the vendor.

3.95   However, this would only require that the financial guarantee amount at the time of the transfer was reflected in the price for the site. The new owner would continue to receive tax relief on any subsequent contribution to the bond. However, no tax relief would be available on rehabilitation expenditure until this exceeded the total balance of the financial guarantee.

Fiscal Incentives to Re-Use Derelict Land

3.96   In order to stimulate the market for derelict land, tax incentives could be given to developers prepared to rehabilitate and re-use such sites. This would be similar in concept to the rates holidays enjoyed in Enterprise Zones. This mechanism could shift the balance more in favour of recycled land as opposed to greenfield sites.

3.97   In practice, sites deemed to be derelict would therefore offer the developer a tax holiday providing that he redeveloped the site. Criteria relating to eligibility would need to be introduced which ensured that such relief actually resulted in a re-use of the site. Nevertheless, such a policy would result in a decrease in the total development costs of such sites which would offset the initial rehabilitation costs that would be incurred.

3.98   The drawback of such an approach would be to provide an incentive to let a vacant site become 'derelict', thereby making it eligible for tax holiday status to incoming developers. As such, the value of developable derelict sites would be artificially inflated, relative to vacant sites. Although such a fiscal measure would redirect investment back into the recycled land market, it would not meet the primary goal of preventing dereliction. **It is not therefore considered further in the evaluation.**

Tax on the Holding of Derelict Land

3.99   A more far reaching use of the tax system would be to consider placing a tax on land that is deemed to be derelict. The key aspects of such a tax are discussed here to illustrate how the tax system could prevent land from becoming derelict. This would involve a considerable shift in current fiscal policy. By introducing a direct financial penalty on landowners holding their land in a derelict state, the tax would provide an additional incentive to undertake rehabilitation or to return the land to a more productive use.

3.100   Derelict land affects the local land market and economy in two ways. The primary effect is that dereliction impedes the redevelopment of the site in question. An important secondary effect is the negative impact of dereliction on adjacent and nearby sites. It is this secondary effect that a tax on the holding of derelict land would address.

Economic Principle

3.101   The principle behind the proposed tax is that the landowner of the derelict site should face the full cost of holding the land in that state. The total costs of dereliction can be separated into:

(i)   the lost potential income of employing the site in the best available alternative use,

(ii)   the external cost of dereliction at that site to those affected by it (eg owners of adjacent land).

3.102   The landowner already bears the opportunity cost of not using the site for an alternative purpose. This foregone income will, in most cases, be less than the cost of actually converting the site to the alternative use. As such, the landowner does not have a financial incentive to rehabilitate the site.

3.103   However, the cost of dereliction to other parties (the externality cost) is not taken into account by the landowner. An economically efficient solution would require him to take into account not only his personal costs and benefits but also those of all the other parties affected by the condition of the site. A mechanism is therefore required by which the landowner will recognise the externality costs of dereliction in order to arrive at the economically efficient outcome.

3.104　A tax on the holding of derelict land would represent this external cost. By imposing these external costs on the landowner, his relative costs of holding the land in a derelict state are increased to those of holding the land in an alternative state (ie vacant or developed for another use). As such, the landowner will have a greater incentive to prevent or remove dereliction.

3.105　It is important to note that by taxing the landowner so that he bears the full costs of dereliction, the decision as to what state to hold the land in remains with the landowner. As such, if the costs of rehabilitation still exceed the total (direct plus external) cost of dereliction then the tax will not provide the landowner with a fiscal incentive to rehabilitate the land. The land will therefore remain in a derelict state which would be an economically efficient outcome under those circumstances. An efficient tax should be exactly equal to the external cost of dereliction.

Tax Assessment

3.106　A tax payable at regular intervals would provide an ongoing incentive to both prevent dereliction and to rehabilitate sites deemed to be derelict. The incentive to landowners to prevent dereliction or to rehabilitate a site would be greatest when the site was assessed for tax purposes. By limiting the period between such assessments, sites would be maintained out of dereliction where it would be economically efficient to do so.

3.107　Using a system of regular assessments and tax payments would also enable additional penalties to be imposed. For example, the tax rate could be increased for sites which remained derelict over a long period of time or where the nature of the dereliction worsened. Regular assessments would also ensure that local authorities had an up to date register of derelict land which could be used for economic development, planning and funding purposes.

3.108　Landowners would have to be able to assess their exposure to this tax liability when their land was still in economic use. This would ensure that they face the appropriate incentives and penalties at all stages of the development lifecycle.

Details of the Taxation Option

3.109　There are naturally key aspects of such an option which would have to be examined in detail. The principal issues relating to the type of tax and how the amount would be assessed are analysed in Appendix H.

3.110　Another aspect of this proposal is the potential for 'hypothecating' the revenue from the tax charge. Tax revenues earmarked in this manner are used in other countries such as the United States and have the effect of making the principle behind the tax clearer and more acceptable. If this were done, those holding derelict land could be contributing directly to a national fund for reclaiming derelict land. This could either be used to supplement–or partially replace derelict land grant funding or could be distributed to local authorities on the basis of the amount of dereliction in their areas.

3.111　**However, the Treasury have strong reservations about the principle of hypothecation and this option is not evaluated further.**

Overseas Experience

3.112　It is instructive at this stage to consider the experience of other countries in preventing dereliction. This section covers policy relating to derelict land in neighbouring European countries as well as the United States and Japan, and demonstrates a variety of approaches taken to dealing with this issue. It is important to note, however, that not all of these mechanisms were introduced to deal specifically with dereliction. In the majority of cases, they form part of a broader framework dealing with land use and development. Nevertheless, there are a range of policy tools which operate to prevent some forms of dereliction.

Germany

3.113   The German planning system does not generally impose rehabilitation conditions on development except for particular categories of use. Certain activities with significant pollution implications are subject to such conditions as well as other forms of regulation.

3.114   The public sector role in rehabilitating derelict land is similarly restricted. Only certain sites in the former East Germany are eligible for partial public funding of up to 90% of the total rehabilitation costs.

3.115   Rehabilitation expenditure is deductible for tax purposes against income. This can be carried back for up to two years to the last year of trading income. Similarly, forward provisions are tax deductible providing that they have been agreed with the fiscal authorities. Both forward provisions and carry back allowances are subject to a limit of DM 10,000,000.

3.116   Property tax is also levied on derelict land providing an additional fiscal incentive to avoid holding land in a derelict state.

France

3.117   Planning permission for development is often accompanied by a planning condition (an "engagement") which can include requirements for rehabilitation and after-use.

3.118   Under a power introduced in 1970 to clear unfit housing, the State can also compulsorily acquire derelict buildings without the need for a public inquiry. Although this power has been extended to include non-residential structures, it is still associated with public health issues and in cases where the owner is unknown.

3.119   Property tax is levied on derelict and vacant land. This ensures that there is no fiscal incentive to mothball sites in a vacant or derelict state.

The Netherlands

3.120   The prevention of dereliction is almost endemic with tight control over development throughout the entire planning system. Emphasis is placed on recycling land with only limited development permitted on greenfield sites. Demolition work is also restricted through building permits, ensuring that a redevelopment plan is in place before demolition can proceed.

3.121   The public sector is prepared to be actively involved in the land market, holding a larger proportion of the land in public ownership than is the case in the United Kingdom.

Denmark

3.122   There is tight control over the development process through the planning system as well as by strategic land acquisition by local planning authorities. This is complemented by a comprehensive register of land ownership which also contains data on key site characteristics. Public authorities are therefore key players in the land development process ensuring that the limited land available is utilised effectively.

Norway

3.123   Norway does not use the same incentives for all types of derelict land but differentiates between those sites that are of cultural, natural or recreational significance. Agricultural and forest land may be restored with public grants but this benefit is only extended to other sites when they are of particular importance.

3.124   Similarly, property tax is only levied on derelict sites which are in themselves a problem; ie located in and around urban areas. No particular incentive is given to site rehabilitation outside these areas. This policy reflects Norway's settlement pattern of relatively densely urbanised centres and sparsely populated regions utilised for forestry and agriculture.

3.125   Tax relief on site rehabilitation expenditure is only available as a deduction from capital gains at the time of the final sale of the land.

Ireland

3.126   There are no public grants available for site rehabilitation of derelict urban sites. However, local authorities can use their Compulsory Purchase Order powers to acquire derelict urban properties. Public grants are provided for up to 30% of the cost of site rehabilitation of derelict agricultural land.

3.127   Tax relief is available for site rehabilitation expenditure relating to agriculture or development in designated areas. This relief is available either at the time the provision is made or it can be carried forward against a future income flow. However, there is no carry-back provision beyond one financial year.

3.128   Furthermore, the Finance Act (1994) restricts tax relief on refurbishment expenses to residential and industrial structures. As such, there is no tax concession for the conversion of sites into office-only premises.

United States

3.129   Public sector grants are generally not available in the US for rehabilitating derelict land. Rehabilitation costs are only tax-deductible to the extent that they are covered by specific depreciation allowances over a property's tax and book lives of approximately 40 years.

3.130   However, if a site is abandoned then its residual book value has to be written off at that time. This loss in value can be offset against present earnings and is therefore a deductible expense. Rehabilitation expenses remain deductible and can be carried back up to three years to the last year of trading income.

3.131   Property taxes are levied by local government and are based on the assessed value of the property. Effectively, if a party holds title to a property then they will be liable for property tax at that site regardless of the condition it may be in. Clearly however, dereliction will be reflected in the assessed value of such a site. These local property tax payments are deductible from federal tax returns.

Japan

3.132   The high demand for developable land in Japan has combined with an extremely fragmented pattern of land ownership to create a considerable issue of land hoarding. The government has acted to prevent land being held vacant in anticipation of future rent increases by levying a vacant land tax to encourage the bringing into use of such land.

3.133   The national land tax is set at 0.3% of market value of the site with exemptions only for specific categories such as nature reserves and strategic sites. In addition, local land taxes of 1.4% are also levied on the basis of a partial value of the land.

3.134   Japan's fiscal land policy is an example of a policy directed not so much at preventing dereliction – there is no public subsidy for rehabilitation–but to tackle wider issues in the land market.

CHAPTER FOUR

Effectiveness of the Options

Evaluation Criteria

4.1   This chapter evaluates the effectiveness of the options to prevent land from becoming derelict. There are a range of criteria that are used to assess each option. In order of priority these are:

1. ***Impact*** *on the Prevention of Derelict Land*
Central to the purpose of the study is the impact that each option has on actually preventing land from becoming derelict. Reducing this flow of land into dereliction can be further analysed in terms of an immediate reduction in the incidence of dereliction and a more sustained reduction over a longer time period.

2. ***Practicability*** *of Implementation and Enforcement*
Under this criteria the degree to which the measures require new administrative, funding and enforcement systems has been assessed. This has also included an assessment of the additional costs incurred and any administrative inefficiencies that may be introduced.

3. ***Incentive*** *on Landowners to Prevent Dereliction*
In order to prevent dereliction, all landowners should have an incentive to either restore their sites or retain them in active use. Such incentives can be achieved through the use of penalties, rewards or a combination of both. The options have therefore been assessed as to the extent that they provide the appropriate incentives on individual landowners to prevent dereliction.

4. ***Flexibility*** *to Local Circumstances*
Although the measures to prevent dereliction should have an unambiguous impact on dereliction, there is also a need for sensitivity to local circumstances. The measures should be providing the appropriate incentives to landowners and this should take the particular site-specific circumstances into account.

5. *Deterrent Effect on* ***Investment***
As the prevention of dereliction involves shifting a rehabilitation liability on to the (private) landowner, this may have a deterrent effect on investment. The degree of certainty as to when and how each measure would be applied by local authorities is of particular relevance here. Each measure has been assessed for its effect on investment and whether this might be displaced to other locations or withdrawn altogether.

6. *Demand on* ***Public Funds***
Shifting more of the responsibility to prevent dereliction onto the private landowner also has implications for the level of public money required to support the measures. Another aspect of the call on public funds is the scale of dereliction that must still be tackled by the public sector and the implications for future levels of publicly funded rehabilitation.

The need for new items of legislation or extensive legislative changes is important when considering the feasibility of the option. Most of these changes would relate to the planning system but there are also potential implications for wider fiscal policy. The scale of legislative changes will be influential in determining the time period over which the options could be implemented and their effect on the flow of land into dereliction.

Rehabilitation Conditions

4.2   The effectiveness of conditions for preventing future dereliction is dependent on their imposition and enforcement by local authorities. It will depend on the presence of conditions which are realistic, robust and well-worded. It will also require local authorities to monitor sites over varying lengths of time.

Impact

4.3   The use of rehabilitation conditions is a proactive measure targeted specifically at the future prevention of derelict land. As such their impact is likely to be slow as they will only be implemented as uses which include them in their planning permission reach the end of their useful life. The benefits are therefore likely to accrue over a considerable length of time.

4.4   Under the current system of legislation, rehabilitation conditions are only likely to work for a limited and specific range of uses such as specialist structures and/or where there is no realistic alternative use for the site.

4.5   Clear guidance would need to be given by the Department of the Environment on matters of implementation, such as rehabilitation standards. This is so that some consistency can be achieved across the country. Even so, there are still likely to be differences in the way authorities impose and enforce conditions.

Practicality

4.6   For specific types of development, the use of rehabilitation conditions is likely to be a practical tool to prevent the occurrence of dereliction. Although the degree of transferability between minerals and non-minerals development is limited, the principle of rehabilitation conditions has been established and the concept is easily understandable.

4.7   The time taken to determine planning applications within relevant categories of development may increase due to additional negotiations between applicant and local authority, and an extra dimension for statutory consultees to comment on. In turn this could lead to a greater number of applicants appealing against non-determination.

4.8   The cost of monitoring and enforcing compliance with conditions, including any subsequent legal action and use of default powers, is likely to rise, and have implications for local authority staff resources.

Incentives

4.9   The incentive on landowners to rehabilitate a site will, to a large extent, be determined by the penalty for non-compliance with the condition (currently a maximum of £20,000 on prosecution for failure to comply with an enforcement notice), the 'cost' to company image, and the ability to raise funds for future projects. Demonstration of increasing awareness of environmental matters is an issue for the property development sector and the more astute businesses and sectors are increasingly interested in guarding their reputations and appearing 'environmentally friendly'.

Flexibility

4.10   Rehabilitation conditions offer the potential for flexibility in their application to individual site requirements. Whilst the idea of a minimum 'rehabilitation' standard was welcomed in responses to the DOE Consultation Paper, detailed discussions with case study interviewees have shown that it would be difficult to implement in practice. Each site would lend itself to different standards of rehabilitation, depending on the type and location of development, and these should reflect local conditions.

4.11   However, in order for this to be achieved, authorities need to have a clear view of the desired end state of a site at the time permission is granted. This is not always possible with 'permanent' development, although it may be possible for 'specific' structures. Industry representatives interviewed in this study recommended a cautious approach since some structures which may not appear to be easily reusable today may become more usable in the future.

4.12   In addition, planning conditions offer some flexibility to deal with changing rehabilitation needs over time. Although authorities have powers to review and change planning conditions, there is a commensurate compensation liability which is likely to give rise to unacceptable demands upon local authority resources. The uncertainty involved in reviewing conditions is also of concern to developers.

Impact on Investment

4.13   Any variation in the use and onerousness of rehabilitation conditions between local authorities is likely to affect locational decisions, particularly of footloose industries. In general terms, the property development sector will look for suitable or the most favourable circumstances in which to develop.

4.14   For most uses, the investment decision itself is unlikely to be affected for two principal reasons: firstly, the risk of incurring the cost of rehabilitation can be discounted over time (ie the likelihood of recycling the land is high); and secondly the cost of any work can be discounted as there is no immediate financial provision to meet the potential future cost of restoration. For marginal uses, the overall investment decision may be affected as such uses may be unable to bear the costs of site rehabilitation.

4.15   Nevertheless, the perception that developers might be deterred from pursuing their applications was sufficient to prevent local authorities in at least two case studies (2.09 and 2.13) from negotiating on rehabilitation conditions.

4.16   A more immediate problem, however, is the likelihood that investors may steer away from developing on problematic or difficult (brownfield) sites, if site reinstatement requirements are applied too enthusiastically here. In particular, in cases where public sector funding is likely to be difficult, finance from other agencies may be difficult to obtain. There is an equity issue associated with the rehabilitation of brownfield sites (with a 'double' cost of site clear up both before and after development) which may deter investment. In case studies 2.03 and 2.12 where retail developers had borne the costs of decontamination and servicing of brownfield sites, the developers felt that it was up to the market to recycle the sites in the future, rather than for them to be penalised with further obligations.

Public Funds

4.17   Rehabilitation conditions would make site reinstatement the explicit responsibility of the applicant. As such they should reduce the need for the public purse to deal with dereliction. They do not contain any safeguards if the operator fails financially. Public expenditure on site rehabilitation is therefore likely to be dependent on the overall level of compliance with such conditions.

Legislative Change

4.18   An initial view is that the imposition of rehabilitation conditions for specific types of built development would not necessarily require a change in primary legislation. The concept is within the bounds of S.70 and S.72 of the Town and Country Planning Act 1990.

4.19   Circular 1/85 would need to be reviewed so that changes in emphasis and interpretation could be introduced. Each of the 'six' tests would need to be reviewed with particular importance being paid to the necessity of a condition, its enforceability and reasonableness.

Financial Guarantees

Impact

4.20 Financial guarantees would clearly provide a reinforcement of rehabilitation conditions. They would ensure that financial provision is made for rehabilitation costs and, as a result, deal with cases of financial failure of the operator. However, in cases of technical failure, arbitration procedures might be necessary to determine whether the actual rehabilitation met the rehabilitation condition requirements. If found to be practicable, financial guarantees in conjunction with rehabilitation conditions could have a more consistent long term impact on preventing land from becoming derelict than rehabilitation conditions alone.

Practicality

4.21 There are significant uncertainties about the willingness of the financial services industry to provide guarantees relating to the rehabilitation of permanent development. Representatives interviewed in this study indicated their inability to assess the degree of risk involved due to the uncertainties of estimating rehabilitation costs and the lack of an established track record. Commercial bonds are usually restricted to investments of less than seven years.

4.22 There would be additional costs for applicants involved in agreeing a financial guarantee and in finalising the legal and financial arrangements. Enforcement costs are also likely to rise, especially to determine cases of technical failure. Legal disputes could pose practical problems.

Incentives

4.23 The cash deposit based form of financial guarantee will provide the greatest incentive for the operator to rehabilitate the site. However, this depends on the costs of rehabilitation relative to the financial guarantee. The incentive would be greatest when the financial guarantee is set higher than the actual rehabilitation costs. If the financial guarantee was substantially lower than the actual rehabilitation costs, then there would be no additional incentive beyond compliance with the original rehabilitation condition, and the benefits of maintaining a good track record.

Flexibility

4.24 The amount of the financial guarantee necessary would depend on the anticipated rehabilitation cost, ie the rehabilitation condition. These would be locally determined and should be sensitive to local circumstances. There are, however, uncertainties in estimating in advance the costs of rehabilitation (see case study no. 1.10). If the system were to be promoted more widely, guidelines should be set regarding the requirement for financial guarantees such that significant cost differentials between operators in the same industry are avoided.

Impact on Investment

4.25 Discussion with the private sector indicated that there was considerable hostility to the use of financial guarantees. However, case studies (such as the windfarm operations) have demonstrated that developers are prepared to provide financial guarantees in certain circumstances. The net impact on investment of financial guarantees therefore depends largely on the type of development and how locationally restricted developers are to a particular site.

4.26 As such, the impact on investment of financial guarantee should be considered on an industry and location specific basis. However, the substantial up front costs of cash-based financial guarantees will dampen investment in all but the most desirable locations. They would also effectively discriminate against small operators unable to provide such funds in favour of larger enterprises.

Public Funds

4.27 Financial guarantees ensure that the operator provides or secures financial resources before the development commences. As such, the public sector would not have to rehabilitate sites at public expense where financial guarantees were in force. Only where there are disputes regarding the rehabilitation standard could public funds be required to complete the rehabilitation.

Legislative Change

4.28 Financial guarantees have been used occasionally by local planning authorities for specific types of development, eg windfarms. In the private coal industry there has been limited use under certain Local Act powers in South Wales. Extending the use of financial guarantees should not involve additional legislation.

Extending Local Authority Powers

Impact

4.29 A new local authority power (based on an extension to S.215 of the 1990 Town and Country Planning Act or under a new section of the Act) to require specified rehabilitation works to a site would act as a threat to landowners and hopefully therefore reduce the flow of new land into dereliction. Its main impact, however, would be as a reactive measure (requiring land to reach a particular state before action could be taken). As such it could have the capacity to tackle existing dereliction, in effect, immediately. It also has the potential to be applied to any type of development in any location, subject to specific criteria being met regarding the condition of the site.

4.30 Assuming that a new provision allowed a notice to be served because a site had become derelict per se (rather than being a harm to amenity) the likely impact on the prevention of dereliction would be limited because land will need to have reached a derelict state before any action could be taken. In addition the potential cost to local authorities of carrying out work in default if the owner fails to comply with the notice or is not traceable may limit the use of a discretionary power.

Practicality

4.31 The experience of S.215 powers is that they offer a limited solution to problems of untidy land. Their use is generally as a "stick" to achieve a desired result but the shortcomings of the existing provision (in terms of grounds of appeal and cost recovery) make them a mechanisms of marginal use and importance.

4.32 There are no overriding constraints as to why a new provision should not be introduced into the Act to focus specifically on the rehabilitation of derelict land.

4.33 Additional financial support would be necessary for LAs to implement this new provision.

Incentives

4.34 In its current form, S.215 of itself provides little incentive for landowners to prevent their sites from becoming 'untidy'. This is due to the discretionary nature of the provision and a calculation of the likelihood of a local authority firstly serving a notice and secondly enforcing it through default powers. As a 'threat' to recalcitrant landowners, the provision is limited.

4.35 Assuming that a new provision successfully addressed the cost recovery issue such that LAs could use the power positively, there would be a greater incentive to prevent land becoming derelict.

4.36 However, there would be little incentive for landowners to prevent land from becoming derelict if the costs of reclamation exceeded the value of the site. In these cases landowners may disregard the notice and leave the local authority to restore land (particularly where the 'owner' has a limited financial interest in the site) unless there was an additional penalty for non-compliance with the notice.

Flexibility

4.37 A new S.215 type power to prevent dereliction offers wide flexibility in the control of sites. Its discretionary nature means authorities could serve a notice on a test of 'expediency' (similar to that for enforcement action against breaches of planning control). It would also allow the authority to specify the steps needed to remedy the situation. These may be the subject of disagreement between the authority and the landowner leading to a varying level and standard of work in different areas. In this context the principle of a 'suitable for use' end state may need to be included in guidance.

Impact on Investment

4.38   Because a new S.215 type power would be discretionary, decisions by footloose investors may be affected by the 'reputation' of local authorities in their use of the power. Concerns were expressed by the business community about generating uncertainty in the land market. However, the various uncertainties inherent in such a provision may ultimately have only a marginal effect on investment decisions if other provisions such as rehabilitation conditions are in force. Nevertheless, discussions with the private sector indicate concerns about enhancing such discretionary powers for local authorities. Investment decisions might reflect the level of activity of the authority in implementing its powers in this regard.

4.39   In addition, landowners holding land in a depressed market where demand for sites was low might be unduly prejudiced by a provision similar to S.215 and liable to default action through no fault of their own or any act of negligence. Some local authorities felt that this would run counter to the principles of public : private partnerships where each party has a positive role to play in bringing sites into use.

Public Funds

4.40   A new S.215 type provision, with a default power for the local authority to take action, has the potential for a high and on-going call on public funds. The recovery of costs particularly on sites requiring significant expenditure on rehabilitation, is likely to meet only part of the outlay by local authorities. A potential area of dispute is likely to be the scope of works and costs associated with them which may be challenged by the owner leading to protracted negotiations and delay in the recovery of costs.

Legislative Change

4.41   The current provisions of S.215 are considered inappropriate and inadequate for preventing land from becoming derelict. Accordingly, a new section of the 1990 Town and Country Planning Act is required. This would need to address the current shortcomings of S.215 in respect of the potential grounds of appeal which should be limited to the need and scope of works (and period of compliance with the notice). The new provision should be accompanied by Regulations to allow a charge on the land to be imposed in cases where a local authority has carried out the works in default and been unable to recover the cost of the works from the land owner.

Tax Relief on Rehabilitation Expenditure

Impact

4.42   Tax relief for rehabilitation expenditure should result in an immediate take-up of the carry-back provision as and when operations ceased on a given site. The effects of a forward provision would generally have a longer term impact.

Practicality

4.43   A precedent has been set for carry-back provisions in the minerals industry. There should therefore be few practical problems related to allowing this form of tax relief on rehabilitation expenditure. Tax relief on forward provisions is not compatible with the current tax regime in the UK, although it is permissible in some other European countries such as Germany and Ireland.

Incentive

4.44   Fiscal relief for rehabilitation expenditure would decrease the costs to operators of rehabilitation. As such, more rehabilitation may be undertaken – thereby preventing extended dereliction – but not through increasing the incentive to actually do so. The financial cost of rehabilitation is simply decreased with the financial return from rehabilitation remaining the same.

Flexibility

4.45   The tax relief measures would be applicable on a nation-wide basis. They would be defined by the type of rehabilitation expenditure allowed for relief rather than by the location of such activity. The scale of rehabilitation works required at a given site and hence the costs on which tax relief would be available would of course be set locally.

Investment

4.46   Taxation relief on rehabilitation would have no impact on inward investment as it lowers the cost of eventual rehabilitation. It may offer some incentive to develop brownfield or currently derelict sites as ex-ante rehabilitation could be offset for tax purposes.

Public Funds

4.47   There would be an unknown loss of tax revenue to the Exchequer from carry-back provisions. The loss may be small but further research is needed to quantify it. There is also the possibility that forward provisions might be used to minimise overall tax liability. This concern could be overcome by limiting such tax relief to cases where a financial guarantee has been agreed.

Legislative Change

4.48   Additional tax legislation would be required to bring carry-back provisions for tax relief on rehabilitation expenditure into line with that provided for the minerals extraction industry. The introduction of tax relief on forward provisions would raise more fundamental issues relating to the principle of tax relief and also require special legislation.

Tax on the Holding of Derelict Land

Impact

4.49   The impact of such a tax if implemented is likely to have an immediate effect on the stock of derelict land by imposing a penalty on the holding of derelict land.

Practicality

4.50   There would be significant practical difficulties to be overcome in enforcing a charge on derelict land. In particular, local assessment would have to be arranged on a regular basis with established criteria. However, there are precedents for assessment of this type under the rating system. There would clearly be a large resource implication in terms of the local assessment process which, to be effective, would have to be repeated at regular intervals.

4.51   Implementation of this option would also involve maintenance of an up to date register of derelict land. This would have resource implications for local authorities.

4.52   A method of distinguishing between vacant and derelict land would be needed. This is central to creating a readily identifiable and stable tax base. The lack of measurable units of dereliction would further complicate the assessment and levying of this tax.

Incentive

4.53   The incentive effect of a tax on the holding of derelict land relies upon introducing a differential cost between derelict and vacant land. If all land not in economic use were subject to such a tax then there would be no incentive effect for the landowner to improve the state of land for which there was no immediate end use.

4.54   The objective of this tax would not be to penalise those landowners who are unable to attract development to their property but to prevent land from being held in a derelict state. By taxing landowners on the equivalent of the external cost of their actions, they would face an economically efficient incentive to prevent dereliction.

4.55   A flat rate charge would approximate to an economically efficient incentive for landowners to prevent dereliction. This would largely depend on how the actual rate were set but, providing that some note is taken of the locational characteristics and type of dereliction, the charge should relate to the externality effect imposed by the site. Landowners would thus be forced to include the external costs of dereliction in their decision as to what to do with the site.

Flexibility

4.56   As the tax would be assessed on a local basis within national guidelines, the charge system would be sensitive to local circumstances. Although it would be important to apply this charge across the whole country, local variation regarding the type of dereliction could be taken into account. Nevertheless, the principle of such a charge should be to encourage the rehabilitation of derelict sites to at least a state where they impose no externalities. The rehabilitation standard required to achieve this state would vary between authorities but the actual charge imposed should continue to reflect the external cost of the derelict state compared to the locally defined neutral, vacant state.

Investment

4.57   Of central importance is the impact of such a tax on the land market. Existing derelict land cannot normally be readily transferred to another owner because of the likely costs of rehabilitating the site to an alternative use. In addition, there is already considerable reluctance in the land market to take on brownfield sites because of potential future environmental liability for existing contamination.

4.58   The imposition of a tax on dereliction would impose an additional liability on the ownership of land that is already derelict. As such the price would have to be adjusted further to represent the additional cost of taking on such a site. As the market price of derelict land is already so low (or even negative) that the market ceases to function, additional liability would shift demand further towards greenfield sites and new development. Speculative demand for derelict sites would be depressed and existing owners would be left with a liability they could only remove through rehabilitation.

4.59   However, new investment is unlikely to be concerned about a tax that would only operate when the operation had ceased. There would thus be an impetus to avoid the land becoming derelict in the longer term. The only category of investment that would be directly affected is speculative behaviour. The acquisition of sites with a view to future development would be discouraged as would speculative building which did not have an assured future. Nevertheless, the latter situation is unlikely to lead to dereliction unless there was a major shift in market demand.

Public Funds

4.60   A tax on the holding of derelict land would result in revenues being generated for the Exchequer. As there is unlikely to be a damaging effect on investment (see above), there should be no offsetting loss to public funds. However, sufficient revenue would have to be raised to offset the administrative overhead of levying on a new tax base.

Legislative Change

The response for most private sector interviewees was that a tax on the holding of derelict land ran counter to the principle of property rights and was therefore unpopular. Essentially a relatively small number of landowners would be affected but the development industry as a whole could also be expected to resist such a move.

Overall Evaluation

4.61   Table 4.1 summarises the main advantages and disadvantages of each of the five options against the evaluation criteria. This indicates that the two options contained in the Government's Consultation Paper – restoration (termed in this report rehabilitation) conditions and extension of S.215 powers – have the potential to assist derelict land prevention.

4.62   Of these, the use of rehabilitation conditions is the more focused towards future prevention but, because of this, its results would only be seen in the longer term. Wider use of rehabilitation conditions would be possible without legislative change but only in clearly defined circumstances.

4.63   A new provision similar to S.215 would provide some threat against allowing land to become derelict and would also enable intervention against derelict land in the shorter term. The steps necessary to introduce such a measure are discussed in the next section.

4.64   Of the two fiscal measures considered, tax relief by way of carry back provisions on rehabilitation expenditure appears to be a workable proposition and could provide some additional incentive to undertake works to prevent land from becoming derelict.

4.65   The final two options – financial guarantees and a tax on the holding of derelict land – would be highly problematic to implement. Without wider experience in the operation of rehabilitation conditions it is difficult to judge the circumstances in which financial guarantees would be required to back rehabilitation conditions. The disinclination of the financial institutions to provide cover for this form of uncertain and long term liability would introduce barriers to entry for new and smaller enterprises.

4.66   A tax on the holding of derelict land would require a major change in fiscal policy, would entail high administrative costs in setting up a collection system, and may penalise certain landowners unfairly. Nevertheless, it would provide an efficient incentive to prevent dereliction and is used in some overseas countries.

Timescales for Achieving Policy Objectives

4.67   The likely impact of each provision in reducing the flow of new land into dereliction is illustrated in Figure 4.2.

4.68   The effectiveness of rehabilitation conditions will only begin to show results when sites covered by such a condition come to the end of their useful life.

4.69   An extension of local authority powers to rehabilitate sites (once enacted) could have an earlier impact on reducing the flow due to the perceived threat that it would introduce. It could also be used as an intervention to reduce the stock of existing derelict land, although to be effective this is likely to result in a considerable call on public funds to cover cases of default action by local authorities, particularly where the landowner or business has failed financially.

4.70   Tax relief on rehabilitation expenditure (once introduced) could have an early impact on reducing the flow of new derelict land unless it could only be applied to new uses. It would not assist reclamation of existing derelict land since it would only be effective for rehabilitation immediately after cessation of the use.

4.71   An early impact could also be achieved following the imposition of a tax on those holding derelict land. However, this option does not fit within the current approach to taxation and therefore is unlikely to be implemented except possibly in the longer term.

TABLE 4.1: EVALUATION BALANCE SHEET

CRITERIA	Rehabilitation conditions financial guarantees	Rehabilitation conditions with powers (revision of S215)	Extension of local authority expenditure	Tax relief on rehabilitation derelict land	Tax on the holding of
IMPACT	**HIGH OVER TIME** — Proactive, but increasing over time as existing planning permissions are superceded.	**LIMITED OVER TIME** — Potential to be effective in cases of financial failure but need not yet established.	**LIMITED IMMEDIATE** — Value as a threat but largely reactive as provision requires site to be in derelict state to invoke.	**LIMITED IMMEDIATE** — Lowers cost of rehabilitation expenditure to landowners but insufficient to significantly prevent derelection.	**POTENTIALLY HIGH** — Threat value. Would encourage land to be kept vacant instead of derelict.
PRACTICALITY	**PRACTICAL** — Appropriate for certain types of development in some situations, but unlikely to be practical in all cases.	**PROBLEMATIC** — Difficulty of securing money and identifying release points.	**PRACTICAL** — Legal and financial support required for local authorities.	**PRACTICAL** — No major barriers to implementation. Limited impact on administrative systems.	**IMPRACTICAL** — Likely to be unpopular. Affects principle of property rights. Significant adminstrative requirements.
INCENTIVE	**LIMITED** — Limited by penalty arising from enforcement and perceived cost to image	**STRONG** — Clear financial incentive to comply with condition but difficult to assess appropriate level of guarantee.	**LIMITED** — Deterent effect limited by grounds of appeal and cost-recovery by local planning authority.	**LIMITED** — Initial uptake likely and would be used where the lower net cost of rehabilitation is sufficient to create a profit incentive to prevent derelection.	**STRONG** — Landowners will take full internal and external costs of derelection into account.
FLEXIBILITY	**FLEXIBLE/SITE SPECIFIC** — Determined by local planning authority and operator on site by site basis. May require national guidelines. Fixed over time once conditions set.	**FLEXIBLE/SITE SPECIFIC** — Determined by local planning authority and operator on site by site basis. May require national guidelines. Fixed over time once conditions set.	**FLEXIBLE/DISCRETIONARY** — Highly flexible to circumstances of site and at discret on of local authority. May require national guidelines.	**FLEXIBLE** — National tax-relief scheme not applied on discretionary basis by local authority but rehabilitation expenditure geared to local circumstances.	**FLEXIBLE** — Local planning authority will assess each site on an on-going basis within national guidelines.
INVESTMENT DETERRENCE	**LIMITED** — Discounting by risk and over time will minimise impact on development generally. Will adversely affect marginal investments.	**DETERRENT** — Increases initial development cost and would have potentially significant deterrent effect.	**UNCERTAIN** — Discretionary nature of provision creates uncertainty for investors but importance in locational/investment decision uncertain.	**LIMITED** — Limited or no impact on inward investment.	**DETERRENT** — Will decrease speculative demand. Should not offset operational sites or plans.
PUBLIC FUNDS	**LIMITED** — Cost of monitoring/enforcement of conditions. Uncertain rehabilitation costs where action in default.	**LIMITED** — Cost of monitoring/enforcement of conditions.	**POTENTIALLY HIGH** — Problem of cost-recovery even if authority able to place charge on land. Potential for protracted legal wrangling.	**LIMITED** — Unknown loss of tax revenues.	**OFFSET BY REVENUE** — Significant cost of assessment, maintaining register, administration and collection. Offset by tax revenue.
LEGISLATION	**LIMITED** — Scope for wider use. Re-emphasis of Circular 1/85 required.	**LIMITED** — Potential exists to extend principle from minerals industry to specific types of development.	**SIGNIFICANT** — Requires drafting of new provision. Provisions largely exist for cost recovery. Grounds of appeal need to be determined.	**LIMITED** — Extension of existing provisions for minerals development.	**MAJOR** — Considerable shift in fiscal policy relating to the taxation of non-income generating assets.

TABLE 4.2: TIMESCALES FOR ACHIEVING POLICY OBJECTIVES

	Immediate	5 - 10 Years	10+ Years
'Restoration' Condition		————————	– – – – –➤
New Local Authority Power	————————————	– – – – –➤	
Tax relief on Rehabilitation Expenditure	————————————	– – – – –➤	
Tax on Holding Derelict Land	————————————	– – – – –➤	

CHAPTER 5

Conclusions and Recommendations

The Concept of Rehabilitation

5.1 Mechanisms to prevent land from becoming derelict could, if implemented, achieve:

- a reduction in the pressure for development on greenfield sites through the reduction or avoidance of 'additional' costs associated with brownfield site development;

- an improvement in the environment, particularly in sensitive areas;

- a reduction in the call on public funds to cover the cost of site rehabilitation.

5.2 The growing acceptance of the 'polluter pays principle' and of the imperatives of sustainable development makes the timing right to consider introducing the concept of rehabilitation of sites more widely into the control of built development. With minor exceptions for special development, the rehabilitation of sites is not explicitly considered in most cases when giving planning permission.

5.3 The concept of restoration is firmly established in the handling of applications for mineral extraction. However, the concept of site rehabilitation is not widely used within the planning system. This can create anomalies at the margins between the minerals planning system and the general planning system, where the same type of development can be treated differently depending on whether it is classed as ancillary to mineral extraction or as non-mineral development. Built development is assumed to be permanent, beneficial, and capable of being recycled by the property market. The stock of derelict land, which represents the legacy left of previous industries shows that this does not always take place.

5.4 It is also clear from looking at a range of recent developments that many local planning authorities do not consider rehabilitation for fear of deterring potential developers and/or investors.

Existing Mechanisms to Prevent Dereliction

5.5 The provisions of the Environmental Protection Act 1990 should reduce the risk of ground contamination from new development and hence help to prevent future dereliction.

5.6 Present planning powers to deal with derelict land, however, are largely reactive rather than proactive. They deal with the problem of derelict land itself rather than preventing the occurrence of derelict land in the first place. Although the normal operation of the development market recycles some derelict land, it is largely central and local government which assists in bringing significantly damaged land back into productive use.

5.7 A central objective of the study has been to look at practical ways that might shift this burden and reduce the flow of new land becoming derelict as well as the call on public funds. The emphasis is therefore on prevention in line with the 'polluter pays principle'. In addition, some of the mechanisms considered may also have an effect on reducing the existing stock of derelict land.

5.8 In order to carry out its task, the study team has looked at mechanisms both within and outside the planning system and sought to assess what potential they offer for dealing with the problem of preventing land from becoming derelict. This has included examining practical examples in the planning field to learn from working experience where possible.

5.9 Finding practical examples has not been easy. This is partly because of the newness of the subject area in conceptual terms but also because the prevention of dereliction is not, in itself, a current planning policy consideration. Whilst regeneration of sites as an end in itself is an objective in the identification of site specific proposals and policies, the prevention of dereliction is not a prime driving force. Local authorities and the development sector are therefore largely unaware of the range and scope of existing tools available and what effect these might have if they were more widely used.

5.10 Having said this, those examples which were found proved highly valuable and encouraging; and assisted with the more detailed exploration of issues. However, there are areas which need further consideration. These form part of the study team's recommendations.

5.11 None of the options examined were able to tackle all aspects of preventing land from becoming derelict. In the case of planning mechanisms, this is not surprising given that these mechanisms were never intended nor designed to deal specifically with this issue. Any benefits for the purpose of preventing dereliction have therefore been secondary to their main function. For financial or fiscal measures, this is because the systems within which they operate only allow them to go so far.

Recommended Measures for Prevention of Future Dereliction

Changing the Climate of Opinion

5.12 It is clear that a change of attitude is required to prevent land from becoming derelict through the development process. The reuse and recycling of land is an important feature in the move towards sustainable development and is also linked to the Secretary of State's quality initiative. **We therefore recommend that:**

* *Government should issue guidance on the use of the planning system to prevent land becoming derelict (eg a redraft of PPG1 and/or PPG12). If new legislation is introduced (see recommendation 13), a Circular on derelict land prevention would assist understanding of the legislation and provide a reminder of existing mechanisms.*

* *Local authorities should be encouraged to discuss rehabilitation/reuse implications of development with applicants at the planning application stage, especially for greenfield development.*

* *Operators/occupiers should be encouraged to consider it part of their responsibility to the community to provide the tidying up of sites and making suitable for alternative use, rather than abandonment when their use ends (this applies particularly where technology and demand patterns change rapidly and development occurs on a greenfield site).*

* *Relevant industry groups, particularly in older industries (eg chemical, petroleum, steel) should be encouraged to adopt rehabilitation practices and instill a stronger environmental conscience through industry codes of practice or conduct.*

5.13 This encouragement to the different sets of actors within the development process could occur, for example, through ministerial speeches and discussions with the relevant associations and interest groups.

Rehabilitation Conditions

5.14 We consider that rehabilitation conditions present the most focused mechanism that the planning system can offer to prevent land from becoming derelict. Such conditions are already being used for certain categories of time-limited development. Rehabilitation conditions would be appropriately applied to developments comprising specialised structures incapable of reuse when the operation ceases, developments with significant environmental effects, and developments on greenfield sites, particularly in rural areas. Local authorities must be seen to enforce against non-compliance of such rehabilitation conditions in order to make the mechanism effective in preventing dereliction.

5.15 The use of these conditions would be less appropriate for development on brownfield sites, especially where the new development is already carrying the costs of improving previously derelict or contaminated land.

5.16 The degree of rehabilitation would need to be defined in each particular case. As a guide, we suggest that the principle of 'suitable for use' should be adopted. The occupier would be responsible for undertaking works to a standard which would allow a similar use to develop the site without additional preparation costs. Thus, any structures on, over, or under the ground would have to be removed and the site made stable. In relation to buildings which could potentially be reused, the objective of the rehabilitation condition would be to ensure that the buildings are kept in good repair.

5.17 **Our recommendations are that:**

* *A wider use of rehabilitation conditions should be encouraged within current legislation and practice for time-limited developments, such as windfarms, telecommunications masts.*

* *The use of rehabilitation conditions should be extended over time to specified types of development, which although not time-limited, would cause problems of dereliction if the use were abandoned. Such developments would include those having significant environmental effects, and also those likely to occur on greenfield, and/or rural locations, such as holiday villages/theme parks, petrol stations, and incinerators.*

* *Planning guidance should be issued to encourage this approach, to include examples of model conditions, and emphasise the importance of subsequent enforcement. Cross references would need to be made as to how the six tests in Circular 1/85 would need to be applied to justify such conditions.*

* *The Department of Trade and Industry should be encouraged to adopt the same line in negotiating consents for power station buildings.*

* *Consideration should be given to amending the GDO, such that operators with permitted development powers to erect specialist structures which are incapable of being reused and are unsightly and potentially dangerous if left abandoned, should consult with local planning authorities on rehabilitation proposals before the use is likely to cease. This could be applicable for example to gas holders and settling tanks on water and sewage works sites. There is already a provision in the GDO in relation to the removal of satellite dishes when they are no longer needed (Class H, Part 1).*

Rehabilitation Conditions With Financial Guarantees

5.18 It is considered that there is insufficient experience yet of the operation of rehabilitation conditions for built development to consider introducing any formalised system of financial guarantees to back such conditions. Financial guarantees are used to a limited extent with highly specialised structures on time-limited consents, eg windfarms. It is appropriate that this is a matter of negotiation between such applicants and the relevant local planning authorities. Clearly there is no point in suggesting a national system of financial guarantees in the short to medium term if the scale of default is minimal and financial institutions are unwilling or unable to participate because of problems in calculating the risks or liabilities.

5.19 **We therefore recommend that:**

* *Any ideas of a more formal system of financial guarantees should be kept under review until experience has been gained on the frequency and seriousness of financial failure or default on rehabilitation conditions for built development.*

* *Any planning guidance that is issued on the subject of rehabilitation conditions should also clarify the circumstances within which financial guarantees are already being used and the financial provisions that have been found to be the most effective.*

Extending of Local Authority Powers

5.20   S.215 powers have a particular purpose in relation to justifying local authority action on the grounds of preserving amenity. They have limited applicability to the issue of preventing land from becoming derelict. Nevertheless, they are another tool in the local authority armoury. **We therefore recommend that:**

*   *The Regulations for which provision has already been made, should be introduced in order that any expenditure incurred by a local authority which has not been recovered from the operator, could be put as a charge on the land.*

5.21   A new section would need to be introduced into the Town and Country Planning Act 1990 to provide a tool specifically geared for use by local authorities to prevent land from becoming derelict. This would allow local authorities to undertake rehabilitation works where the landowner was unknown or failing to take action. **We therefore recommend that:**

*   *A new provision should be introduced into the Act similar to S.215 but to carry out rehabilitation works allowing entry onto private land deemed derelict.*

*   *This new provision should allow the cost of the rehabilitation works to be charged back to the landowner and placed as a charge on the land.*

Tax Relief on Rehabilitation Expenditure

5.22   The ability of mineral operators to offset restoration expenditure incurred within three years after cessation of trade against the trading income of the final accounting period, provides an incentive for rehabilitation to take place after operations have ceased. **We therefore recommend that:**

*   *Consideration should be given to introducing legislation to allow carry-back provisions on rehabilitation expenditure incurred within three years after the cessation of trade.*

Tax on the Holding of Derelict Land

5.23   This form of tax penalty is used in several overseas countries but is not in line with the UK tax regime. There would be administrative hurdles to its implementation and the equity implications would need to be carefully thought through. In practical terms, a system would need to be set up in order to differentiate between vacant and derelict land. **We therefore recommend that:**

*   *Further detailed research should be undertaken on the practicalities and impact of implementing a tax on the holding of derelict land, before considering it as a long term possibility.*

Timescales for Implementation

5.24   A final consideration is the timescale for introducing any necessary changes into the planning system in order implement the recommended measures. The timescale within which any measure would have an impact on reducing the extent of new dereliction following its implementation, was considered in Section 4.7.

5.25   Suggested timescales for implementing policy and legislative changes related to each of the mechanisms considered are shown in Table 5.1.

5.26   We are confident that a higher profile could be given to the concept of rehabilitation through the use of the existing planning system, to run alongside environmental protection powers. This would require awareness-building amongst the different actors within the development process.

5.27   Nevertheless it would be necessary to introduce legislative changes to provide more focused powers to prevent legislation. Such powers should be introduced gradually in order to overcome the innate conservatism of the property industry and financial markets.

5.28   The need to overcome inertia and resistance to change is by no means unique nor insurmountable. A similar shift in thinking and approach was accommodated in the minerals field with the more widespread use of restoration conditions in the 1960s. Local financial and regulatory systems have adapted to the restoration obligations required under the Private Acts in South Wales for controlling private opencast coal operations (introduced in 1987 but with a forerunner in Mid Glamorgan in 1973), including attendant financial guarantees.

5.29 Changes need to be capable of practical implementation and acceptance, in principle, by affected parties. Their introduction would also need to be subjected to adequate prior consultation with affected parties, and when implemented, be accompanied by clear guidance to local authorities on the use of new powers, for example through a Circular on derelict land prevention.

Table 5.1: **Timescales for Implementing Policy Changes**

| | TIMESCALES | | |
Action/Provision	Short	Medium	Long
'Restoration' Conditions	• Apply more widely to specifiedactivities on time-limited permissions	• Issue planning guidance cross referenced to Circ 1/85 • Extend scope of activities to be covered	• Consider amending GDO in respect of utilities development
Financial Guarantees		• Monitor levels of default on 'restoration' conditions ducing a system of guarantees	• If default a problem consider ways of intro-
S.215 and New LA Power	• Introduce Regulations for LAs to put a charge on the land to recover their costs under existing S.215	• Amend legislation to introduce new section allowing prevention of dereliction as an objective for LA action	
Tax Provisions	• Amend legislation in respect ofcapital allowances and carry back provisions		• Consider tax on derelict land

APPENDIX A

Research Specification

Introduction

A1   The Government places considerable importance on the reclamation and re-use of derelict land. As well as improving the environment, reclamation provides sites for new industrial, commercial and reclamation development, and thereby relieves pressure on green field sites.

A2   Despite the achievements of local authorities and the private sector in reclaiming land, the rate at which the stock of derelict land in England has been reduced remains slow, as new land is becoming derelict all of the time.

A3   The Department has recently been paying out more than £100m a year in DLG to tackle this problem. The Welsh Development Agency is currently spending around £30m a year on land reclamation.

A4   The scale of the derelict land problem and the cost of the DLG programme have prompted interest in finding mechanisms to prevent dereliction from arising in the first place. The National Audit Office 1988 report "Department of the Environment: Derelict Land Grant" found that the closure of major industrial activities other than mineral operations (eg large factories, steelworks or chemical point) could be a significant cause of dereliction, and questioned the justification that these have to be restored by the public purse rather than at the owners' or operators' expense.

A5   In 1992 the Department of the Environment and the Welsh Office issued a consultation paper "Proposals to Prevent Land Becoming Derelict". Broadly, this sets out 2 options:–

   (a)   Applying restoration conditions to new planning permissions for industrial or commercial use, similar to those routinely attached to minerals workings.

   (b)   Extending local planning authority powers to require the owners and occupiers of land to reclaim derelict land, eg by building on existing powers under S.215 of the Town and Country Planning Act 1990.

In general terms these proposals were given a lukewarm welcome by local authorities and amenity bodies, whilst industry was worried that these proposals (particularly the application of restoration conditions) might add to their costs and thereby deter new investment. Some responses also raised other practical questions, such as defining when land had become derelict and defining the sort of standard to which it ought to be restored.

Aims

A6 The aim of the research is to follow up this consultation exercise and examine whether the planning system can be used to prevent non-mineral sites from becoming derelict. The research will:–

(a) assess the effectiveness of the various options for using the planning system to ensure that restoration takes place, and the costs that they would impose upon industry.

(b) advise the Department on how any such options might be implemented.

Objectives

A7 The research team will:–

(i) prepare a preliminary assessment of the various options for using the planning system to prevent dereliction, both in terms of their effectiveness in preventing dereliction and of the cost which they might impose on industry

(ii) carry out a series of case studies of derelict and reclaimed sites to examine how the application of any of these options might have affected the outcomes

(iii) assess the extent to which the tax system might help or inhibit restoration obligations imposed through the development control system

(iv) evaluate the overall costs and benefits of options

(v) advise on how any preferred options might be implemented, indicating whether any legislative changes would be needed and what sort of Departmental advice might be required.

Responses to 1992 Government Consultation Paper

Overall Response

B1   The Consultation Paper was issued by the Department of Environment in February 1992, with responses sought by May 1992.

B2   The document was circulated to a limited audience of some 80 bodies comprising environmental groups, professional bodies and interest groups, local government associations, development corporations, industrial associations and individual companies. Local authorities and the Department of Trade and Industry were not included on this list, however the Consultation Paper was printed in the April 1992 Bulletin of the Encyclopedia of Planning Law.

B3   A total of 76 responses were received. 50% of the responses were from bodies not on the original circulation list. A full list of respondents is given below.

B4   In early 1992, proposals regarding contaminated land were also being circulated, leading to some confusion regarding the distinction between derelict and contaminated land. Many of the responses also focused on the reclamation of land, rather than the prevention of dereliction. The analysis below covers solely the latter. It summarises the overall reaction of different categories of respondent, and comments on each of the two options put forward in the Consultation Paper, namely:

- Option 1 : Restoration Conditions
- Option 2 : Extension of Section 215 powers.

Analysis of Response

Environmental Organisations

B5   Total number of respondents in this category: 10.

B6   Environmental organisations were unanimous in their general support for both the proposals. There was no significant preference of one option over another as many regarded them as complementary.

B7   General issues raised:

- Policy on derelict land prevention should be combined with provisions in the Environmental Protection Act (1990).

B8 Option 1 issues:

- More land uses should have restoration conditions applied than implied in the Consultation Paper.
- Financial guarantees should be required in respect of restoration.
- Restoration should be in line with local conditions, perhaps through a two-stage process. There is considerable pressure here for using derelict land as semi-natural wildlife reserves.

B9 Option 2 issues:

- No position is taken on appropriate funding mechanisms.

Professional Organisations/Interest Groups

B10 Total number of respondents in this category: 11.

B11 Widespread support for the proposals, with only one respondent failing to endorse Option 2 and two-thirds support for Option 1.

B12 Option 1 issues:

- More land uses should have restoration conditions applied than implied in the Consultation Paper.
- Restoration should be in line with local conditions.

B13 Option 2 issues:

- Of the seven respondents expressing an opinion, five argued that the local authority should be able to recover the full reclamation cost from the landowner.

Local Government Associations

B14 Total number of respondents in this category: 7.

B15 Widespread support for the proposals, with no explicit dissent.

B16 General issues raised:

- The existing grant structure relating to derelict and contaminated land should be reviewed.

B17 Option 1 issues:

- More land uses should have restoration conditions applied than implied in the Consultation Paper.
- Financial guarantees should be required in respect of restoration.
- There are potential problems with the implementation of restoration conditions regarding the uncertain timescales and multiple occupancy of large sites.

B18 Option 2 issues:

- A third of the respondents felt that increased Derelict Land Grant would be required to support practical implementation of expanded S.215 powers.
- Several respondents mentioned the need to improve legal procedures to enable local authorities to use the expanded powers. Current powers are not utilised fully due to lack of financial and legal support.
- A third of authorities mentioned the possibility of using Compulsory Purchase Orders to effect the reclamation of derelict land and thereby simplify the recovery of expenditure.
- Opinions on funding formulas were divided.

Local Authorities

B19   Total number of respondents in this category: 14.

B20   Widespread support for the proposals, with only Rotherham MBC rejecting Option 2.

B21   Option 1 issues:

- Financial guarantees should be required in respect of restoration.

- Support for the two stage restoration process.

- The English authorities were split evenly between including more land uses, or restricting the land uses which would face restoration conditions under Option 1.

B22   Option 2 issues:

- No dominant issues arising.

Development Corporations

B23   Total number of respondents in this category: 7.

B24   Widespread support for the proposals, with unanimous support for Option 2.

B25   Option 1 issues:

- Identifying potential dereliction from land uses is complex in the case of non-mineral developments.

- More land uses should have restoration conditions applied than implied by the Consultation Paper.

- Restoration should be in line with local conditions.

B26   Option 2 issues:

- Three of the development corporations felt that increased Derelict Land Grant would be required to support practical implementation of expanded S.215 powers.

Industry Associations

B27   Total number of respondents in this category: 8.

B28   Only 50% supported the proposals generally, with a marginal preference for extension of S.215 powers as a last resort. Both options were rejected by at least one organisation.

B29   General issues raised:

- A practical definition of derelict land is required.

B30   Option 1 issues:

- Identifying potential dereliction from land uses is complex in the case of non-mineral developments.

- Non-mineral developments have uncertain termination timescales.

- Three of the organisations rejected financial guarantees, primarily because of their impact on costs.

- A quarter of the respondents argued for a minimum standard of restoration.

- The British Retail Consortium, contrary to expectations, argued that there should be no negative impact on inward investment as a result of adopting restoration conditions.

B31   Option 2 issues:

- Extension of local authority powers was regarded as unnecessary by the UK Petroleum Industry Association.

- Five of the remaining bodies supported the idea of expanding local authority powers, subject to a right of appeal.

Industry/Property Owners

B32   Total number of respondents in this category: 14 (including consultancies).

B33   Less than 50% supported the proposals generally, with over 50% rejecting the concept of expanding S.215 powers. Half of the respondents accepted the case for restoration conditions.
General issues raised:

- Several respondents were concerned that property owners should not be responsible for dereliction caused by previous land uses.

- Incentives (eg tax deductions) should be available to reclaim land/prevent dereliction.

B34   Option 1 issues:

- Non-mineral developments have uncertain termination timescales.

- Two rejections of the concept of financial guarantees and no positive acceptance.

- Over a third of respondents argued that restoration conditions would have a negative impact on investment.

B35   Option 2 issues:

- Outright rejection of extension of local authority powers by over half of the respondents in this group.

- Requirement for higher Derelict Land Grant (similar to argument for incentives).

Department of Trade and Industry

B36   Although not on the original circulation list, the DTI did provide a brief response to the consultation. Their primary concern regarded the impact of the proposals on investment in Britain. The DTI is keen to prevent Britain becoming uncompetitive, especially as regards other European countries. Mention was made of potential European-wide policies regarding derelict land.

List of Respondents

Group 1   Environmental/Conservation Organisations
  Open Spaces Society
  Countryside Commission
  RSPB
  English Heritage
  Joint Countryside Advisory Service
  Royal Society for Nature Conservation
  National Society for Clean Air and Environmental Protection
  CPRE
  National Trust

Group 2   Professional Bodies/Interest Groups
  Institute of Civil Engineers
  RIBA
  Landscape Institute
  RICS
  RTPI
  TCPA
  National Planning Forum
  Chartered Institute of Building

National Housing and Town Planning Council
CIPFA
Institute of Surveyors, Valuers and Auctioneers

Group 3   Local Authority Federations
Federation of Economic Development Authorities
Association of Metropolitan Authorities
Association of District Secretaries
District Planning Officers Society
ADC
Council of Welsh Districts
Assembly of Welsh Counties

Group 4   Local Authorities
Walsall MBC
Cumbria CC
Langbaurgh BC
Stoke on Trent
Dartford BC
Liverpool City Council
Rotherham MBC
Bolton MBC
Macclesfield BC
North Bedfordshire BC
Gwynedd CC
Gwent CC
Dyfed CC
Mid Glamorgan CC

Group 5   Development Corporations
Sheffield DC
LDDC
Leeds DC
Central Manchester DC
Trafford Park DC
Welsh Development Agency
Land Authority for Wales

Group 6   Producer Federations
British Ball Clay Producers Federation
British Retail Consortium
British Property Federation
National Federation of Clay Industries
BACMI
UK Petroleum Industry Association
CBI
Federation of Small Businesses

Group 7   Industry/Property Owners
British Gas
English Estates
Anglian Water
British Coal
British Waterways
British Railways
Powergen
Grosvenor Laing Urban Enterprises Ltd
ICI
Lord Falmouth's Estate

List of Interviewees

Local Authority Associations:

Assembly of Welsh Counties[1]
Association of County Councils
Association of District Councils[1]
Association of Metropolitan Authorities[1]

Authorities/NGOs:

Northumberland CC
Gwynedd CC[1]
Langbaurgh BC[1]
Stoke on Trent BC[1]
Bedford DC[1]
Walsall MBC[1]
Rotherham MBC[1]
Sheffield Development Corporation[1]
Welsh Development Agency[1]
English Partnerships

Institutions/Amenity Groups:

RTPI[1]
RICS[1]
Town and Country Planning Association[1]
Civic Trust
UK Environmental Law Association

Industry Associations:

British Property Federation[1]
Water Services Association
Chemical Industries Association
UK Petroleum Industry Association[1]
Confederation of British Industry[1]

Financial Institutions:

Inland Revenue
Lloyds Bank
Hambros Bank
Hogg Insurance Brokers
ECS Underwriting

Scotland (by Telephone):

Scottish Enterprise
Glasgow District Council
Strathclyde Regional Council
Lanarkshire Development Agency
Highlands and Islands Enterprise

TOTAL INTERVIEWS = 34

[1] Denotes original respondent to 1992 consultation

Interview Checklist

Aide Memoire for Interviews Conducted in Stage 2 of the Study

Introduction

- The purpose of this interview is to discuss measures which might prevent land from becoming derelict.

- Are you aware of the Government's Consultation Paper "Proposals to Prevent Land for Becoming Derelict" published in February 1992?

- If you did not respond, why not?

- If you did respond are there any additional comments you might wish to make at the outset?

- What types of development do you feel are likely to cause dereliction problems in the future?

Restoration Conditions on Applications

The use of restoration conditions formed one of the options included in the consultation paper. Employed in the minerals extraction industry, restoration conditions could potentially be applied to other industrial and commercial developments.

- What other types of land / developments do you think might be appropriate for the extension of restoration conditions? Certain (or all) industrial developments? Commercial development?

- Such a system of restoration conditions would require an operational definition of when land becomes derelict. What do you regard as being derelict land?

- Should the land be restored to its 'original' condition?

- If restoration conditions are imposed should the standard of restoration be determined by the developer, the planning authority or by negotiation between developer and the planning authority?

- Should there be some minimum standard of restoration (for example, to a soft-end use)? Should these be nationally or locally determined?

- Is there some merit for allowing for a two-stage restoration process to minimise deadweight loss (ie redundant restoration) incurred in restoring to hard end use without a prospective use for the site. Could restoration conditions deal with the first stage of restoration?

- Should the restoration condition be limited to meeting a one-off restoration standard or should an "after care condition" also be considered to allow for further steps to be taken after the initial restoration (such as planting, fertilising and draining)?

- Should the restoration conditions be reviewed to take account of changed circumstances after a finite period of time? This would affect only the restoration standard rather than the principle of the actual development. Conditions could thus be modified to either a greater or lesser standard. If accepted, what should this time period be; 10 years, 20 years?

- Further to changing circumstances, if buildings are designated as listed or subject to conservation orders, how would the restoration obligation be fulfilled?

- Should a restoration scheme be set out or left for agreement nearer the time, thereby imposing an open-ended liability on the landowner/developer?

- Would there be a deterrent effect on investment if restoration conditions were introduced on planning permissions?

- For industry; how do you assess the discounted cost of future restoration liabilities and how are they provided for in the accounts?

- Should there be a separate appeal process related to the restoration condition in addition to the appeal process already in existence for other conditions on planning permissions?

- Should the freeholder be liable where the land reverts from the leaseholder? If so, should this apply retrospectively to leasehold agreements already in existence?

Restoration Bonds

- Do you think that the concept of a restoration 'bond' is feasible for all or certain types of development?

- Should the bond cover the full cost of restoration or allow for restoration in the case of default by the last owners of the development?

- How might you measure the amount of the future restoration cost and hence the size of bond required?

- Should the future restoration cost (and hence bond) be reassessed during the life of the development?

- How do you think the bond system might operate: a contribution to a bond in a lump sum on completion of the development or by instalments?

- Would you regard the availability of tax relief as sufficient incentive to make financial provision for future restoration of industrial property? If not, would the existence of a tax penalty on derelict land as well, or on its own, be required?

Extension of S.215 Powers to Require Restoration

The second option in the original consultation document concerned extending existing local authority powers to allow reclamation to proceed where the land owner was unknown or failing to take action.

- For Local Authorities: what experience do you have in the use of S.215 powers? What lessons emerge for their extension?

- Is the use of such power justified where amenity considerations (as under existing S.215 powers) do not apply?

- If it is justified, then under what circumstances should local authority action be initiated against a landowner?

- Do you consider that the powers available to local planning authorities under S.215 would need to be strengthened if they were to be used to tackle dereliction?

- Should the owners be charged for the recovery or part recovery of the costs and if so what should be the basis for this:
  — recovery of the total cost of reclamation?
  — recovery of the notional element not covered by grant (formerly DLG), as if the land owner had undertaken the reclamation?

— recovery equal to the increase in the value of the land?

- What might the resource allocation implications be for your organisation / client group?

- Would there be an impact on private sector investment to voluntarily undertake land reclamation, with or without the assistance of grant?

- Would there be any impact on investment because of the existence of these powers, or is the future so heavily discounted?

- Should permitted development be included under these powers?

- Are procedures for appeal necessary in addition to those under S.217 that protect development not in breach of planning control unless it is in an unusually unsightly condition?

- To what extent could the extension of local authority powers to reclaim land be seen as complementary to the options for restoration conditions on certain types of planning application?

The Tax System and Derelict Land Prevention

An alternative option to those listed above is to impose a tax on the holding of derelict land.

- Is there any merit in considering the direct use of the tax system as a threat against allowing land to become derelict?

- What might the definition of derelict land be as the basis for taxation?

- What would be the most appropriate tax base:
  — market value?
  — book value?
     estimated reclamation cost?
  — something else?

- At what rate might the tax be levied?

- Should any such tax apply to derelict land only, or be extended to vacant land as well?

- Should any such tax be raised locally or nationally?

- Should any such tax be hypothecated so that the revenue could be used to fund:
  — grants for private sector land reclamation
  — tax relief for land reclamation

Use of Compulsory Purchase Order (CPO) Powers

Proposed by RICS and supported in the consultation response by the RTPI, FEDA and WDA this option would facilitate local authority intervention in derelict land. A number of questions are raised:

- What should be the basis for compensation to private owners particularly in areas of low demand? RICS suggest 10% above market value, would you agree with this?

- Would there be an incentive to reclamation if compensation was set at below market value?

Other Concepts

- Should local authorities be obliged to keep an up-to-date register of vacant and derelict land (both in public and private ownership) to assist incoming developers? This may provide an incentive to owners to market land as it becomes derelict. How would local authorities undertake and provide the resources for this ongoing exercise?

- Should local authorities include derelict land or potentially derelict land in the schedules attached to Local Plans?

APPENDIX E

Case Study Selection

Range of Case Studies

E1   The issues investigated in the study were forward looking, namely the mechanisms that might prevent land becoming derelict. It was therefore necessary for the team to consider existing types of development which may be difficult to reoccupy when the original use ceases, and whether lessons from the past could usefully be applied in the future.

E2   The aim of the case studies was to get wide coverage of issues rather than a strictly representative sample. Overall, 40 case studies were undertaken, divided between three groups.

E3   Our initial proposal had envisaged undertaking two groups of case studies. However successful interviews, especially with local authorities at Stage 2 of the study, had highlighted the potential for a third group. This group consisted of recent developments where existing mechanisms were already being used to prevent future dereliction (either intentionally or unintentionally). The other two groups comprised recent development where mechanisms had not been used but where dereliction may be an issue in the future; and sites abandoned by previous development which had remained derelict for a considerable length of time. Details of individual case studies are found in Appendix F.

1.   Case Studies Involving Mechanisms to Prevent Dereliction
Particular emphasis was placed on this group. It offered the greatest potential for understanding why provisions had been made, how they worked in practice, and whether or not alternative mechanisms had been considered.

2.   Case Studies Involving Recent Development Without Provisions
The focus for this group was forward looking, rather than retrospective. Given that developments had gone ahead without any provision for preventing future dereliction, emphasis was placed on testing the likely levels of acceptability of different measures if these had been imposed.

3.   Case Studies Involving Derelict and Recently Reclaimed Land
This group was used to explore the circumstances under which land becomes and remains derelict, and the effectiveness of planning mechanisms in dealing with dereliction retrospectively. It had also been hoped to explore how planning mechanisms might have prevented the sites from becoming derelict but in most instances development had taken place so long ago when circumstances were very different, that this was not possible.

Selection of Criteria

E4   The choice of case studies within the three groups was made using the following criteria:

- **range of development types** including current developments which could lead to future dereliction such as telecommunications towers, windfarms, power stations, waste incinerators; major new industrial plant; hi-tech business parks, retail and leisure schemes. Housing was, however, specifically excluded as it was felt that housing land is readily recycled;

- **range of geographic areas** including representation from each region within England, and from Wales. In addition one case study was included at the Steering Group's request from Scotland.

- **range of mechanisms** to give a good balance of examples where planning conditions, legal agreements, Section 215, financial guarantees had or could have been used.

E5   In addition, a balance was sought between different planning regimes to include development which had gone ahead under normal planning procedures and that which had gone ahead under permitted development rights.

E6   The identification of particular cases was based on examples that were raised in the Stage 2 interviews, ideas provided by Steering Group members, and the Consultants' previous project experience.

E7   The geographical distribution of case studies within the three groups is shown in the following table.

Case Study Checklists

Derelict Land Prevention and the Planning System

Case Study Checklist

Group 2 (New and Recent Developments) – Developer/Owner/Operator

Introduction

The purpose of the interview is to assess the impact that the proposals to prevent land from becoming derelict would have on the viability of recent developments. The discussion should cover the background to the original decision to locate at the site as well as the implications of the proposals on this decision.

Background information

Site name:

Date: Researcher:

Site owner:

Operator:

Interviewee:

Position:

Type of development:

Date planning permission granted:

Date site became operational:

Local planning authority:

Brief description of the site

Who is the owner of this site?

What is their relationship with the operator and developer?

What are the terms of the leasehold contract (if applicable)?

Section A – Location decision (COMMON TO ALL CASE STUDY TYPES)

1. When did your organisation locate at this site? [   ]

2. What were the factors influencing your location decision:
    - local knowledge
    - labour supply
    - transport links
    - availability of land
    - market for product
    - location of suppliers
    - availability of government grants
    - other

3. Was this originally a greenfield site?   YES/NO
    - if YES, was this a key factor?   YES/NO
    - if NO, were the existing structures retained?   YES/NO
    - if NO, who paid for the restoration cost?
      - A) Previous owner
      - B) Current owner
      - C) Public funds
      - D) Combination of the above
      - E) Other

4. What role did public agencies play in attracting you to this location?

5. What alternative locations did you consider?
    - Were any of these sites overseas?   YES/NO

6. Is the operation at this site a new start or a relocation from elsewhere?
    - A) New start
    - B) Relocation
      - If a relocation, what determined the relocation?

Section B – Planning permission (COMMON TO ALL CASE STUDY TYPES)

1. Did the local planning authority attempt to impose any planning conditions that were not accepted?   YES/NO

2. If YES, what were these conditions?

3. Did you enter into any S106 planning agreements at the time of application?   YES/NO

4. If YES, what do these entail?

66

5. If YES, what combination of factors led you to agree to these provisions?

7. Do you have any experience at other sites of accepting and/or implementing these conditions/legal agreements?

8. How did the financier of this development react to the use of these mechanisms to prevent dereliction?

9. Are there any other areas of environmental/health legislation which limit your use of this site? (e.g. Environmental Protection Act/Water Resources Act)

Section C – Use of the site (COMMON TO ALL CASE STUDY TYPES)

1. What is the estimated life-span of your operations on this site?

2. If applicable, what do you anticipate will be the subsequent use;
   A) Same   (different operator)
   B) Similar   (conversion of existing structures)
   C) Other commercial   (no reuse of structures)
   D) Soft end use
   E) Depends on market
   F) Don't know

4. If you do cease operations here, what alternative use could be made of the site <u>and</u> remaining structures?

5. Do you regard the existing use of this site as being likely to inhibit subsequent use of this site for other end uses?   YES/NO

6. If YES, what particular aspect of your use of this site would impede future use?

Section D – Outline of the study issue

For the purposes of this study, the working definition of dereliction is the existence of redundant structures on a site preventing further use of that site. In essence, the removal or conversion costs of these structures outweigh the net economic benefit of using the site over an alternative location.

The proposals that are being considered involve placing a responsibility on landowners to remove such structures from the site once their use has ceased.

For the purposes of this interview, we have estimated the restoration costs as a percentage of the initial development costs. As such, a simple retail structure would cost 2.5% of its original development costs to remove. However, a complex use with extensive underground workings may cost up to 15% of the original development cost to restore.

The requirement to restore the site could be introduced as an additional planning condition when development permission is granted as is currently the case in the minerals extraction industry.

The use of restoration conditions would in effect impose a liability on landowners to remove those structures they had constructed after their use had ceased. By allowing a grace period, the site could be sold to another owner with the structures remaining but the restoration liability would follow with the ownership of the land. Naturally, any subsequent planning permission on that site would revise the restoration conditions in line with the new use.

1. How would a restoration cost estimated at 2.5% – 15% of your capital costs affect your decision to invest in this particular venture?

   A)   Not at all

   B)   Marginal effect

   C)   Significant effect

   D)   Decisive factor – would not proceed with investment

2. If D), then where would your investment be directed?

   A)   Other UK location

   B)   Other European location

   C)   Other worldwide location

   D)   Expand other site

3. If you still continue with the investment decision, how would you provide for this additional future liability?

   A)   As a development cost

   B)   As an ongoing revenue cost

   C)   One off capital payment

   D)   Other

4. Would this future liability be heavily discounted?   YES/NO

5. How would you deal with the additional cost represented by the restoration liability?

   A)   Absorb as an additional cost

   B)   Pass on through product price

   C)   Discounted over time so as to be negligible

6. How would the imposition of restoration conditions affect your competitive position vis a vis other firms?

   A)   Not at all

   B)   Marginal effect

   C)   Significant effect

7. How would the funding institution regard the restoration liability in terms of financing this development?

   A)   Not at all

   B)   Marginal effect

   C)   Significant effect

   D)   Decisive effect

8. Who would bear the ultimate costs of the restoration liability in this case?

   A)   Developer/operator

   B)   Funding institution

9. If the local planning authority required a higher restoration standard beyond that set out in the minimum national standard, would you consider locating elsewhere in the UK?   YES/NO

    Assuming that restoration conditions are to be imposed, some form of financial guarantee could be required to ensure that the liability is covered.

11. What impact would a requirement to provide a financial guarantee have on your investment decision:

    A) Not at all

    B) Marginal effect

    C) Significant effect

    D) Decisive factor – would not proceed with investment

12. If you were required to provide a financial guarantee to the value of the estimated restoration cost, how would you achieve this:

    A) Deposit (from reserves)

    B) Revenue

    C) Bank guarantee (eg bond)

    D) Other

    E) Don't know

13. If some form of insurance could be provided whereby the insurer would provide the guarantee in the event of default for a premium, would this be an attractive option?   YES/NO

Section F – Extension of local authority powers under S215

The alternative proposal to prevent dereliction is to enhance local planning authority powers under S215 of the 1990 Town and Country Planning Act. This would give local planning authorities the power to restore land deemed to be derelict and to charge this cost back to the private landowner.

1. If authorities had these enhanced discretional powers (subject to the usual right of appeal), how would this affect your assessment as to the risk of locating in this area?

    A) Not at all

    B) Marginal effect

    C) Significant effect

    D) Decisive factor – would not proceed with investment

2. Do you feel that the use of this discretional power would have a different impact on your operational decisions relating to the site than the current power of local authorities to compulsorily acquire land?

Derelict Land Prevention and the Planning System

Case Study Checklist

Group 3 (Derelict and Recycled Sites) – Local Authorities

Introduction

This paper outlines the areas to be covered in the case study interviews with private landowners and/or site operators for derelict and recycled sites.

The purpose of the interview is to assess the impact that the proposals to prevent land from becoming derelict would have had in preventing dereliction or altering the outcome of market recycling of land. The discussion should cover the factors leading to the dereliction of the site as well as the implications of the proposals on the final outcome.

Background information

Site name:	
Date:	Researcher:
Local planning authority:	
Interviewee:	
Position:	
Current owner:	
Current state:	
Previous owner:	
Previous active use:	
Date site became derelict:	
Length of time site derelict:	

Background

1. Brief description of the site including:

    - location

    - access

    - physical description

2. Brief description of the development:

3. Who is the developer of this site:

    A) owner-operator

    B) owner-developer

    C) leasehold-developer

    D) leasehold-operator

    E) other

Section A – Factors leading to dereliction

1. What were the primary factors causing this site to become derelict?

    A) Decline of entire industry

    B) Decline of particular area

    C) Financial failure of operator

    D) Relocation of operator with no replacement

    E) Property market

    F) Planning related reasons

2. Once the primary use had ceased, did any marginal uses locate there for relatively short periods of time?   YES/NO

3. If YES, what types of uses (and company structure) did locate there?

4. Under what ownership structure was the site when it became derelict?

5. Were any attempts made at the time to prevent dereliction and attract new uses?   YES/NO

6. If YES, please give details.

7. Were any difficulties encountered in tracing the owner of the derelict site?   YES/NO

8. Which method of tracing the owner was eventually used (eg land registry) and how much did this cost?

Section B – Action taken after site became derelict

1. Was any action taken once the site was derelict to reuse the site?   YES/NO

2. If YES, please give details.

3. Did the local authority attempt to undertake any action at this site under S215?   YES/NO

4. If YES, did this succeed and were any problems associated with the use of this instrument?

5. If NO, why not?

6. Did the site remain under the same ownership structure as when it actually became derelict?
                                                                                            YES/NO

7. If NO, how did the site transfer title to another owner?

8. Is there any evidence of interest in the site from the private sector that would allow reuse of the site within the next 2 years?   YES/NO

9. Does the existence of dereliction at the site impede reuse or development of the site and/or neighbouring sites?   YES/NO

Section C – Tools to deal with and prevent dereliction

One of the proposals being considered is the introduction of new legislation that would give local authorities the power to enter land that they deemed to be derelict, undertake restoration and to charge the cost back to the landowner. This would involve some of the same principles as lie behind the existing legislation in S215 of the 1990 Act.

1. If DLG were to be replaced by such a measure, would it have any impact on creating incentives to prevent dereliction?

2. Would your local authority be prepared to carry out restoration works under such legislation to ensure that this had the desired impact on incentives?

3. Could such works be implemented with due regard for particular circumstances and features which might involve leaving part of the site vacant because of listed buildings?

4. How would such a provision impact the transfer of title over land that had been restored? Would the charge on the land speed up the development process?

5. What would be the impact on your economic development strategy of entering land under contentious circumstances?

6. Do you regard this measure as preferable to the use of CPO?

APPENDIX G

Summary of Case Studies

Group 1: Case Studies of Existing Mechanisms

1.01 PROPOSED WINDFARM, NORTHUMBERLAND

INTERVIEWEES:	Local Planning Authorities Developer/Applicant
CURRENT STATE OF SITE:	Commercial forest
PREVIOUS SITE/BUILDING CONDITION:	Undeveloped woodland
DATE OF PLANNING PERMISSION:	Application not yet determined
MECHANISMS TO PREVENT DERELICTION:	Restoration condition and financial guarantee

1. This is an application for a 80MW wind farm, currently awaiting approval by the DTI. (The scale of development means that the determination of the application is outside the jurisdiction of the local planning authority). The site is in a remote but exposed location, close to the Northumberland National Park and visible from Hadrians Wall, a World Heritage Site.

2. The view of local authorities consulted on the application is that the sensitive location justifies the imposition of a restoration condition to cover decommissioning of the turbines, including site rein-statement. Negotiations are currently taking place on the use (and appropriate level) of a financial guarantee, details of which are confidential.

3. From the local authority's perspective, the use of restoration conditions and a financial guarantee would ensure that the precedent of development is not established on the site and that the land will be returned to its natural state should the wind farm use cease. In this case the local planning authority is able to negotiate from a position of relative strength on the agreements. There are only a limited number of alternative sites available to the developer and the environmental sensitivity of the area is acknowledged by all parties.

4. Any legal agreement would be between the local planning authority, the developer and the owner, Forestry Enterprise. It is likely that the applicant would develop the site and sell it on to a power generating company. In this eventuality, the successor in title will be obliged to accept the obligation under the terms of this 3-way legal agreement.

5. **The applicant's experience on other sites suggests that where a financial guarantee is provided it is normally accounted for by the company as an additional cost met by revenue from the site (ie income from the sale of power generated at the site) and the scrap value of the turbines. It is estimated that the cost of decommissioning, if required, would be less than 0.5% of the capital cost of the project.**

1.02 CHALET DEVELOPMENT, RUSHPOOL HALL, SALTBURN

INTERVIEWEES:	Langbaurgh Borough Council
CURRENT STATE OF SITE:	Holiday Chalets
PREVIOUS SITE/BUILDING CONDITION:	Grounds and garden to Rushpool Hall
DATE OF PLANNING PERMISSION:	Full planning permission, September 1987. This is not a time-limited consent
ESTIMATED LIFE SPAN OF OPERATIONS:	Ad infinitum
MECHANISMS TO PREVENT DERELICTION:	Restoration condition

1. From the mid 1980s onwards, Langbaurgh BC has sought to encourage tourism as part of an overall economic regeneration strategy. At that time, the authority commissioned a study by consultants, John Brown, to identify areas of tourism development. Rushpool Hall was identified as an area of expansion and although the authority would not normally have granted planning permission in such a sensitive location, it did so on the basis of consultant's recommendations.

2. As a result, the authority felt it was necessary to attach conditions to the permission for the chalet development to safeguard the site on amenity grounds. The prevention of dereliction per se was not considered. The condition was not negotiated and the authority's view was that there was a remote chance that it would need to be implemented. It has not been possible to trace the original owner to assess any difficulty which may have occurred in connection with the imposition of condition.

3. Since its development, the site has changed hands several times. The permission was originally issued to the freehold owner of the land. Since this time the freehold of the site has changed hands twice and each chalet has been leased to private individuals.

4. **The authority now considers that the condition attached to the planning permission is weak as it is poorly drafted and ambiguous. The condition makes provision for the removal/demolition of chalets and reinstatement of the land to its former use once the chalet site has ceased to operate. The local authority has no powers to deal with the effect of abandonment/dereliction of individual lessees. Based on their own previous experience, the authority estimates that it would cost approximately £170,000 (based on current prices) to implement the condition (£20,000 for administration, £150,000 for site clearance and site reinstatement).**

1.03 SOUTH CRAMLINGTON DISTRIBUTION CENTRE, NORTHUMBERLAND

INTERVIEWEES:	Northumberland County Council Arthur Andersen S.C.
CURRENT STATE OF SITE:	Distribution centre
PREVIOUS SITE/BUILDING CONDITION:	Opportunity site
DATE OF PLANNING PERMISSION:	10 December 1986
MECHANISMS TO PREVENT DERELICTION:	Financial guarantee

1. This strategic site was entirely owned by Northumberland County Council who intended to develop it for light industrial uses. A complex agreement was made with a developer, Norfolk House, for the development of the site in 9 phases. In return for preparing the whole site and providing access roads and services across all the phases, Norfolk House would receive full title to the first phase. However, before such time Northumberland County Council would retain title over the entire site until the services had been provided.

2. In the event, Norfolk House went into receivership. As the site preparation and servicing had commenced but not been completed, Northumberland County Council retained full title. Norfolk House's receiver, Arthur Andersen, was unwilling to release the investment sunk into the site and needed to realise the asset value of that investment quickly. As a result, the receiver and Northumberland County Council agreed that title on the first phase could be transferred providing that there was an undertaking by the receiver that the servicing of the site would be completed.

3. As part of this separate agreement, Northumberland County Council required a form of financial guarantee to ensure that the work would actually be completed. The cost of the outstanding work was therefore calculated and a cash based financial guarantee of £108,400 was lodged by the receiver for that amount. In the event that works were not completed by the receiver, the guarantee would revert to the County Council. The site was serviced as agreed in the original contract between Norfolk House and Northumberland County Council and the guarantee was returned to the receiver.

4. **This case study illustrates how financial guarantees can be effective in binding an agreement. By providing such a guarantee, all parties can be assured that the agreed actions will be taken or the sum of the guarantee be made available as compensation. Central to this approach is that the bond amount must accurately reflect the costs of undertaking the work so that all parties face the appropriate incentives.**

5. **In practice, the fact that both parties to the above agreement were dependent on each other was instrumental in over-coming the difficulties in negotiating the financial guarantee. For the purposes of preventing dereliction, the substantial up front cost of financial guarantees would act as a disincentive to development, especially if alternative sites were available where no such guarantee is required. However, in the County's view, in cases where the developer has few alternative locations, there is a definite potential for seeking a financial guarantee to ensure restoration.**

1.04   KIRKLEATHUM WALLED GARDEN, LANGBAURGH

INTERVIEWEES:	Langbaurgh Borough Council
CURRENT STATE OF SITE:	Partially repaired
PREVIOUS SITE/BUILDING CONDITION:	Grade II* walled garden: poor condition
DATE OF PLANNING PERMISSION:	n/a
SITE SIZE:	0.01 ha
ESTIMATED LIFE SPAN OF OPERATIONS:	Ad infinitum
MECHANISMS TO PREVENT DERELICTION:	Repairs Notice

1. This case study illustrates the use of a Repairs Notice for preventing further deterioration and eventual dereliction of a Grade II* listed structure. The authorisation of the Notice was sufficient to prompt action and the case never reached the stage where a Compulsory Purchase Order was served on the owner by the local planning authority.

2. During 1991 Langbaurgh Council was authorised to serve a Repairs Notice on the owner of an 18th Century walled garden. The walls had fallen into a poor state of repair and the authority wished to prevent further deterioration. As the listed walls were not attached to any property, there was little financial incentive for the owner to maintain the structures. Hence the walls had not been maintained.

3. The act of notifying the owner of authorisation to serve a Repairs Notice was sufficient to prompt the owner into releasing the land before the Repairs Notice was actually served. The authority were therefore able to purchase the site from a willing owner and carry out remedial works. The cost of restoration was approximately £40,000.

4. The Council had been particularly interested in the structure because of its listed status. Had the walls not been listed, they would have allowed it to deteriorate further to dereliction.

5. **The Council found the powers afforded to them in respect of Repairs Notices useful. They viewed them as being beneficial tools. They were considered more flexible and easier to administer than the alternative use of a S.215 Notice being served on the owner. Particular issues raised in relation to S.215 related to standards of restoration. In particular what standard should a building, or in this case, the garden walls be restored to given that the owner would have no say in the standard of restoration but would have to pay for the works? Additionally, what administrative costs would be involved in following up payment from the owner? This would be a difficult task and, in some cases costs, could escalate if the case had to be pursued through the magistrates court.**

1.05 HOLIDAY VILLAGE SITE, MULLAN PARK, CHESTERFIELD

INTERVIEWEES:	Chesterfield Borough Council
CURRENT STATE OF SITE:	Under construction (abandoned)
PREVIOUS SITE/BUILDING CONDITION:	Derelict structures on part of site and flytipping. Some authorised material storage
DATE OF PLANNING PERMISSION:	Various
MECHANISMS TO PREVENT DERELICTION:	S.215 Town and Country Planning Act 1990

1. The site was originally used for open cast mining and restored for leisure use. Planning permission was granted in 1975 for the provision of a cricket field, pavilion and car park. During the mid 1980's temporary consents were granted for the storage of materials on part of the site, but subsequently enforcement action was taken against the site's unauthorised use for this purpose and flytipping.

2. In 1983 outline planning permission was granted for a new use of the site (holiday village) and reserved matters submitted and approved in 1986/87. Only part of the permission was implemented re the access roads and the site subsequently abandoned. The Pavilion which had existed since 1975 was never cleared.

3. In 1990 a Dangerous Structures Notice was served on the owners of the site requiring the demolition of the former cricket pavilion which had fallen into a dilapidated state. In 1990 authorisation was also sought under S.215 for clearance of the tipped material from the site and this subsequently included material from the demolished pavilion.

4. The local authority faced difficulties in locating the owner of the site to recover the cost of the works following the financial failure of the company owning the site. However, through the Land Registry they were able to trace the mortgagees of land. Following delay to allow the site owner or their agents to carry out the work, the mortgagees undertook to cover the local authority costs in carrying out the work plus administrative charges. These included the demolition of the building under the Dangerous Structures Notice and removal of debris and material from the site as specified in the S.215 Notice.

5. **In this case study the interests of the mortgagee in being able to dispose of land which was both unfettered by any outstanding Notices and in a reasonable state were crucial to the successful recovery of costs. Without this interest, the costs may not have been recoverable.**

1.06 ELECTRICITY TRANSMISSION MAST, PEAK DISTRICT

INTERVIEWEES:	Peak National Park Authority
CURRENT STATE OF SITE:	Operational
PREVIOUS SITE/BUILDING CONDITION:	Moorland
DATE OF PERMISSION:	February 1992 (Temporary)
SITE AREA:	Negligible
ESTIMATED LIFE SPAN OF OPERATIONS:	5 years
MECHANISMS TO PREVENT DERELICTION:	Dismantling and Reinstatement Conditions

1. This case study illustrates the use of time-limited consents in conjunction with dismantling and reinstatement conditions. Although the principle reason for attaching conditions to this development is on amenity grounds, the authority is aware that such conditions may help to avoid dereliction in the future.

2. During 1992, an application was submitted to the Peak National Park Authority by an electricity company for a transmission mast. The development proposed was sited in a particularly sensitive and exposed location. The authority therefore decided to grant permission subject to conditions. In addition, they were of the view that permission should be temporary to maintain flexibility. Permission was therefore granted up to and including the end of 1996.

3. A condition was imposed on the permission requiring the mast to be permanently removed from the land and the site reinstated to its former state at the end of the permission period unless an application for an extension had been approved by the authority.

4. No specific "standard" of restoration was set but, with hindsight, the authority felt they could have done more to spell out exactly what was required.

5. Due to the location and specific nature of the development, no objections were received from the developer. They viewed the condition as reasonable given the development's sensitive location.

6. The authority's approach is, where possible, to prevent the retention of structures or buildings in sensitive locations once their original justification has ceased to exist. In the case of the electricity transmission mast this was because the permission was granted for a specific use only and no other development would have been accepted.

7. **The authority has previous experience of similar telecommunications structures where such conditions had been imposed. They are also increasingly using dismantling and restoration conditions in rural isolated locations to remove farm buildings no longer required. This is in line with a policy contained within the recently approved structure plan.**

1.07   IPSWICH HOSPITAL MEDICAL WASTE INCINERATOR

INTERVIEWEES:	Suffolk County Council
CURRENT USE OF SITE:	Medical waste incinerator
PREVIOUS USE OF SITE:	Medical waste incinerator
DATE OF PLANNING PERMISSION:	18 October 1993
MECHANISMS TO PREVENT DERELICTION:	None

1. A medical waste incinerator was built at Ipswich Hospital under Crown Immunity in 1984. However, provisions introduced under the Environmental Protection Act (1990) requiring a higher standard of operation, prompted the need to replace the incinerator by 1996.

2. The Regional Health Authority decided to centralise the incineration of medical waste to one location. The Ipswich site was therefore chosen as the location for the new incineration facility after an extensive evaluation process. Central to the scheme was the re-use of the existing incinerator structure, especially the 49 metre chimney. Although the new incinerator has three times the capacity of the original, the daily throughput is still below the threshold requiring regulation by HMIP. Suffolk County Council therefore act as both waste regulation authority and planning authority.

3. Planning issues raised at the site were primarily concerned with additional traffic flows and nuisance for local residents. Planning conditions were agreed which related to the actual operation of the site only.

4. Despite the relatively short life span of incinerators (around 10-15 years) it was anticipated that incinerator facilities would always be provided at this location. As a result, the future dismantling of the incinerator facility did not figure prominently in the planning process. The Regional Health Authority had made a strategic decision to locate at that site. The future of the site is thus felt to be assured by the commitment of the Regional Health Authority to a regional incinerator facility.

5. The County Councils' view is that should the incinerator cease to operate, the site can be recycled for an alternative use. In the opinion of the County Council, urban sites will be redeveloped over a period of time as there is likely to be an alternative use for those sites. Restoration conditions are considered to be more appropriate for sites and developments for which there is no potential after use or where the costs of re-using the site would be extremely high. Only in these cases (predominantly highly specific developments) should restoration conditions be imposed to prevent dereliction.

6. A further point relates to the restoration of such sites without a specific end use. This could result in the destruction of valid structures (for example, the 49 meter chimney of the previous incinerator) and result in ongoing costs being incurred in the maintenance of cleared sites.

7. **This case study indicates that conditions requiring restoration to a previous use should only be imposed where the development process is unlikely to be able to redevelop a site after the use in question has ceased.**

8. In the case of urban development, even where it is of a highly specific nature, the land market and the development process is unlikely to leave sites derelict over long periods of time. Clearly, highly contaminated sites do present additional problems but these issues should increasingly be controlled through provisions under the Environmental Protection Act (1990).

1.08   VACANT OFFICE BLOCK, CENTRAL LONDON

INTERVIEWEES:	LB Camden Bob Colenutt, LB Barking & Dagenham
CURRENT STATE OF SITE:	Occupied office building
PREVIOUS SITE/BUILDING CONDITION:	Unoccupied office building
MECHANISMS TO PREVENT DERELICTION:	Punitive rates on vacant property

1. When completed in the 1960's, Centre Point was in a prime central London location. At that time, the property market was rising and expected to continue along an upward trend. As such, the owners did not let the building on any long term leases, preferring to leave it empty until the property market was closer to peaking and leases could be sold for a higher price. The property was vacant for a number of years and even squatted at one point.

2. Before the introduction of the Uniform Business Rate, local authorities levied rates on commercial properties. Rates were generally not levied on vacant or derelict buildings. In normal market conditions, it would not have been "reasonable" to levy rates on empty buildings. In these circumstances, land owners would normally be seeking to attract tenants and would not be penalised further. However, when the property market was rising, speculative developers and property owners were waiting before releasing their buildings onto the market so as to ensure the maximum return; ie when the property prices were highest.

3. When this occurred at Centre Point, the London Borough of Camden took the view that this projected a negative image of the Central area given that it was physically dominating the core retail and office area of the West End. As such, Camden took the route of applying punitive rates – charging rates on the empty building as if it was occupied. Although this action was not widespread amongst local authorities, it did prove to be effective in this case. The owners of Centre Point leased out the space to offset the costs of paying rates on the empty building. The additional tax burden therefore served to change the balance of costs in favour of bringing the building into active use.

4. However, other local authorities faced problems in applying punitive rates on empty buildings. Property owners were generally in a strong position to argue that such action was unreasonable due to either the lack of demand or because insufficient time was allowed to let out or occupy the building. The 1974 recession saw a rapid decline of the property market and removed the incentive to speculate on property. Punitive rates were therefore not the appropriate tool to encourage occupation of buildings. The local authority power to levy punitive rates was abolished in 1979.

1.09 OIL EXTRACTION, WYTCH FARM, DORSET

LOCATION:	Sensitive coastal area
INTERVIEWEES:	Operator
CURRENT STATE OF SITE:	Operational
PREVIOUS SITE/BUILDING CONDITION:	Greenfield; AONB, SSSI
DATE OF PLANNING PERMISSION:	1986
SITE SIZE:	Extensive
ESTIMATED LIFE SPAN OF OPERATIONS:	25 years (with options to renew)
MECHANISMS TO PREVENT DERELICTION:	Restoration conditions and strategy

1. Key points raised in this case study are the negotiating process and financial provision by the operator to carry out restoration works.

2. The development comprises the extraction of minerals in a sensitive coastal area. Permission for development was granted in 1986 and, as with all mineral developments, the permission was time limited. Over 300 planning conditions were attached to the planning permissions. The applications were accompanied by an Environmental Impact Assessment.

3. The location specific nature of the development had meant that it was particularly important for the operator to establish early consultations and a professional working relationship with the minerals authority to assist the mineral applications through the decision process. This was particularly important given the site's sensitive location. A significant number of meetings and discussions took place between the operator and the authority prior to a decision being made. Early discussion helped to highlight potential issues of concern, including operational constraints such as noise, pollution control, visibility and reinstatement of the site, and this enabled site specific conditions to be addressed. This meant that when permission was granted, there were no conditions that could not reasonably be implemented by the operator.

4. **Although a formal fund has not been set up, the operator is setting aside funds as part of the revenue generated to pay for future decommissioning and reinstatement of the site. During the period since permission was granted, the operator has continued to address issues of decommissioning and restoration. The operator has volunteered and is working on a restoration strategy to address different types of habitat land use, and quality of restoration appropriate to various development sites.**

1.10 COALCLOUGH WIND FARM, BURNLEY

INTERVIEWEES:	Burnley BC Renewable Energy Systems Limited (operator)
CURRENT STATE OF SITE:	Operational
PREVIOUS SITE/BUILDING CONDITION:	Unimproved rough grazing
DATE OF PLANNING PERMISSION:	Full planning permission granted 3.7.92. Permission time limited
SITE SIZE:	Stretching to a length of 1.5 kilometres
ESTIMATED LIFE SPAN OF OPERATIONS:	15 years (as specified on the planning application)
MECHANISMS TO PREVENT DERELICTION:	Restoration conditions and sinking fund

1. This is a newly constructed wind farm on high lying rough grazing land. The land is designated an Area of Special Landscape. Conditions have been attached to the planning permission to overcome concerns of visual blight in the event that the wind farm ceases to operate.

2. An earlier application by the same applicant had been refused in September 1991 (despite an officer's recommendation for approval) on the grounds that it would have unacceptable environmental effects. In particular, it would conflict with interim policies adopted by the Council to govern the control of wind energy developments. Although the application was always envisaged as being time-limited due to the short lifespan of wind turbines, no conditions had been recommended to deal with dismantling of structures. As a result, councillors refused the application as they were concerned about the possibility of derelict turbines left standing in this sensitive location once operations ceased.

3. After permission was refused, the developer/operator took the initiative. Public meetings were held by the developer to explain the development and explore concerns. Once the issue of future dereliction had been identified, the developer entered into detailed negotiations with the local planning authority. The developer had previous experience in Cornwall (a wind farm also operated by Renewable Energy Systems Limited) where restoration conditions had been used. In the Cornwall example, £20,000 had been set aside by the company to pay for dismantling of the structures. These terms were offered to the local planning authority.

4. **The local authority used the conditions attached to the Cornwall application as a framework for devising their own conditions suitable to the Burnley case. These involved the removal of all development above ground level; the moorland soil reinstated within 12 months; and the dismantling of any turbine generator which remained out of normal operations for more than 12 months.**

5. **However, they felt £20,000 would be insufficient to cover dismantling costs and requested a sum of £40,000 which was agreed by the developer. A condition stating that an inflation-indexed bank bond be provided for this sum was therefore included.**

6. The developer's view had been that, as with minerals, wind farms could only be developed in specific locations. They had therefore been prepared to offer assurances in order to make the development more acceptable. In addition, the sum requested was small in comparison with the future anticipated revenue (ie £10m). For the developer, the only difficulty had been providing money up front rather than as revenue once the site was operational. However, a bank bond could not be secured. The developer and local authority therefore set up a joint building society account. They agreed that the money would be available to the Council to carry out decommissioning in the event of default. If the operator restored the site to the reasonable satisfaction of the local authority then the whole amount and any interest incurred would be repaid to the applicant or its successors in title.

7. **Renewable Energy Systems Limited and Burnley Borough Council are members of the British Wind Energy Association. The Association has recently published best practice guidelines for wind energy development. The guidelines state that decommissioning and land reinstatement are normal practice and advise that these are usually covered either in planning conditions or by planning agreement.**

1.11 HYDRO-ELECTRIC SCHEMES, SNOWDONIA

INTERVIEWEES:	Gwynedd County Council
CURRENT STATE OF SITE:	Undeveloped (3 Sites)
PREVIOUS SITE/BUILDING CONDITION:	Vacant/agricultural
DATE OF PLANNING PERMISSION:	Not yet determined
MECHANISMS TO PREVENT DERELICTION:	Restoration Condition

1. Gwynedd County Council has jurisdiction over planning applications within the Snowdonia National Park boundary. This includes a number of applications for hydro-electric schemes.

2. Proposals for hydro-electric power generating schemes have been submitted in three locations. These comprise two new developments and reinstatement of a previously approved but abandoned scheme. Applications for development generally involve new turbine buildings, weirs and underground pipework. Development associated with electricity lines (ie poles and cables for carrying electricity supply) are governed by different legislation and involve applications to the DTI with a notification to the local district council.

3. To date planning permission has not been granted for any hydro-electric schemes requiring the removal/decommissioning of plant approved under a planning permission. An application near Bethesda was eventually refused although prior to the decision, discussions had been held with the applicant regarding the removal of weirs and turbine housing on cessation of the use. A draft condition included two main provisions: the permission would have been 'temporary' (for 60 years, the design lifespan of the structures), but if before that date the turbine ceased to operate for not less than 12 months, then the weirs, turbine house and transformer compound (and all other structures on or above the ground) would have to be dismantled and materials removed from the site. Decommissioning would have to take place within three months of the expiry of the permission/cessation of the operation.

4. A similar condition is being considered for two current applications near Blaenau Ffestiniog and Llanberis. In all cases the rationale for the condition is to protect the environment and visual amenity rather than preventing dereliction per se. Whilst the structures were considered acceptable in planning terms (being of stone and slate construction) being located in an area of environmental sensitivity and high visual amenity, the local authority were seeking the removal of visible man-made/artificial structures if the operation ceased.

5. **In the draft conditions, the local authority was also seeking to achieve a high standard of restoration including environmental benefits over and above the demolition of the structures. This would have included reinstatement of the ground rather than leaving a hard standing.**

6. **Some form of financial guarantee (referred to as a 'bond') to cover the cost of decommissioning these was considered unnecessary given the nature of the applicant (a major power generating/supply company). However, a legal agreement (including provision for financial payments to cover monitoring of the environmental effects of the development) has been considered for this type of development.**

1.12   OIL TERMINAL, DYFED

INTERVIEWEES:	Dyfed County Council Pembrokeshire Coast National Park
CURRENT USE OF SITE:	Landscaping of redundant area of oil terminal
PREVIOUS USE OF SITE:	Oil terminal facility
DATE OF PLANNING PERMISSION:	1970
MECHANISMS TO PREVENT DERELICTION:	Voluntary restoration agreed with operator

1.   Attempts have been made to employ restoration conditions in respect of oil related developments in the Milford Haven area. A planning approval for the extension of an ESSO refinery granted in July 1970 sought to include the following condition:

"In the event of the use of any part of the land for industrial purposes being permanently abandoned the Company (ESSO) shall remove the buildings and structures erected thereon and restore the part of the land concerned to agricultural use to such reasonable extent as may be agreed by the County Council, or, in default of agreement, determined by the Secretary of State."

2.   This condition was recognised by the local planning authority as being "a novel condition in relation to industrial development in Pembrokeshire" and was not accepted by the applicant as it represented an open-ended commitment which could entail very large expenditure in removing substructures and importing quantities of soil in order to allow future agricultural production.

3.   Although formal restorations conditions were not imposed on the planning permission, the operators of the oil terminal (ESSO) have carried out restoration works on part of the site where the operational use has ceased. Thus, in 1990 planning permission was sought to undertake earthworks and landscaping within part of the oil refinery complex in order to restore the area to a natural state. This formed part of an on-going programme of works intended to remove evidence of previous refining activities, with the final aim of establishing a natural landscape having wildlife potential. Although these restoration works were not required by conditions on the planning permission, they were imposed voluntarily by the site owner/operator.

4.   **This example points to the possibility of restoration arising from voluntary action by an operator, perhaps arising from an internal code of good practice. In instances such as this it is clearly in the interests of the operator to maintain good environmental practice (especially as this site is within a National Park) in order not to jeopardise future developments.**

Group 2: Cast Study of Recent Developments with No Rehabilitation Provisions

2.01 ELECTRONIC COMPONENTS PARK, CLEVELAND

INTERVIEWEES:	Cleveland County Council, Economic Development Department
	Stockton-on-Tees Borough Council
	Hartlepool Borough Council
CURRENT STATE OF SITE:	Not yet developed
PREVIOUS SITE/BUILDING CONDITION:	Greenfield
DATE OF PLANNING PERMISSION:	November 1994 (outline application)
ESTIMATED LIFE SPAN OF OPERATIONS:	Ad infinitum
MECHANISMS TO PREVENT DERELICTION:	None

1. The case study highlights the reluctance of authorities to impose restoration conditions on permanent development unless there are overriding reasons to do so. In this case, due to the exposed and greenfield location of the development, the authorities would have liked to have imposed some form of reinstatement condition on the site. However, fears of 'frightening the developer off'; the lack of use of restoration conditions for permanent development; and difficulty of conditions meeting the six tests of Circular 1/85 caused restoration conditions not to be imposed.

2. The international developer has recently bought 200 acres of land with an option to buy an additional 200 acres to construct an Electronics Components park. The site is well connected, with easy access to the A689 and A1(M), and is split between two Boroughs.

3. The region within which the site lies is severely depressed with high rates of unemployment. Local authorities in this area therefore place particular emphasis on economic regeneration and the encouragement of employment generating industries. In addition, several incentive packages are offered as a means of attracting inward investment.

4. During 1992, the County Council became aware that the electronics company were undertaking a series of site appraisals within the region with a view to develop. One of these included a large 400 acre greenfield site to the north of Billingham. Liaison meetings were therefore set up early on in the process with the developer to discuss development incentives and options. The county council became aware that the electronics company were undertaking a European-wide site search. Much had to be done to try and 'win over' the developer. Given that the development would provide approximately 3,200 jobs, an economic assistance package amounting to some £10m was assembled by the Economic Development Department of the County Council. Assistance in the Cleveland case included a dedicated TEC to recruit and train staff at all levels for the electronics component development. Similar packages were being proposed by European authority counterparts as a means of attracting development.

5. The overriding economic benefit of this high profile development was seen as outweighing environmental disadvantages. The development was therefore informally treated by both local authorities as a departure from policy and outline permission was granted.

6. The view of the authorities was that negotiations were delicate and the developer could pull out at any time – indeed they may do so in the future as proposals are still at a relatively early stage. They therefore needed to be cautious in their approach. Hypothetically, although the authorities felt they may have been in a strong position to request some form of reinstatement of the site, they felt wary of piloting such conditions on this site in particular. They were especially aware of potential difficulties with Circular 1/85 and the lack of similar conditions being used elsewhere in the country for permanent development.

2.02 NELSON PARK INDUSTRIAL ESTATE, CRAMLINGTON NEW TOWN

INTERVIEWEES:	Blyth Valley District Council English Partnerships
CURRENT STATE OF SITE:	Industrial Estate
PREVIOUS SITE/BUILDING CONDITION:	Greenfield. Specifically allocated in the New Town Plan
DATE OF PLANNING PERMISSION:	Full planning permissions obtained for site on 18.12.90 and 21.11.89
SITE SIZE:	Under 20 ha
ESTIMATED LIFE SPAN OF OPERATIONS:	Ad infinitum
MECHANISMS TO PREVENT DERELICTION:	No planning mechanisms. However, lease agreements offer potential

1. The case study illustrates the potential of alternative mechanisms outside the planning system for preventing dereliction. Potential is offered through lease agreements between English Partnerships, the owners of the site, and the leasees of individual workshop units.

2. Full planning permission was given by Blyth Valley District Council with normal planning conditions. At the time permission was granted the imposition of conditions to prevent dereliction was not considered. Even today the imposition of such conditions on similar development is considered unreasonable by the authority. Their view is that such conditions would suppress the market and be a deterrent to developers. Similarly, English Partnerships would find the imposition of such conditions unreasonable. Already they operate on land that has little or no prospect of take up by private developers operating in isolation. The imposition of conditions would place further constraints on encouraging development from their perspective.

3. However, as freeholders, English Partnerships are willing to negotiate with leaseholders when returning buildings. English Partnerships operate full repair leases with short terms leases lasting for 14 or 24 years and long term leases lasting for a period of 125 years. On long term leases, they accept that it may not be practical or possible for leasees to return buildings in a full state of repair. An alternative would therefore be to return a vacant site back to English Partnerships with buildings removed, although this is not offered automatically and is negotiated between freeholder and leaseholder.

2.03 RETAIL PARK, ROTHERHAM

INTERVIEWEES:	Stadium Group, Rotherham Borough Council
CURRENT STATE OF SITE:	Operational
DATE OF PLANNING PERMISSION:	Planning permission not required. Date of construction 1992
PREVIOUS SITE/BUILDING CONDITION:	Brownfield
SITE SIZE:	8 ha
ESTIMATED LIFE SPAN OF OPERATIONS:	Ad infinitum
MECHANISMS TO PREVENT DERELICTION:	None

1. The site lies within Rotherham's Enterprise Zone. Submission of a planning application and granting of planning permission were therefore not required prior to site development in 1992. As a consequence the local planning authority had had little contact with the developer and was unable to comment on details of the application.

2. The site is located on former slag tips and lies on the northern edge of Rotherham. The site had lain derelict for a number of years and interest was shown in its development only after it had been declared part of the Enterprise Zone. Development of the site formed the first phase of a much larger mixed retail proposal.

3. One of the questions asked by consultants during interviews was how the authority would have responded if provision had been made (eg in the GDO) to require restoration of the site at some date in the future. Although officers of the authority welcomed the idea in principle, they were unsure about what effect this might have on investment decisions. In addition, they felt the development was a significant improvement on previous land uses: it had upgraded the area, and had served to draw additional inward investment into the town of Rotherham. Their overriding view was that the developer had successfully transformed a derelict site into one that could easily be recycled by the land market.

4. Similar views were expressed by the developer. The developer, who was also the freeholder of the land, had not been able to obtain DLG or similar grant money to assist with site works. Their view was that the requirement to reinstate or restore land at some time in the future was both inappropriate and would most likely have prevented them from developing the site in the first place. They would have been unable to bear the cost of site remediation works before development commenced and restoration costs at some date in the future.

5. The developer was essentially just the freeholder. Individual lease agreements had been set up for each retail outlet and the investment had then been sold on to a Trust. Fragmentation of interest in the land and loss of control by the freeholder would make it difficult to implement any restoration conditions on the site. In addition, the developer's view was that the site could always be used for something. They intended retaining the site and could develop it for other uses if necessary at a later date.

2.04 POWER STATION, KEADBY, SCUNTHORPE

INTERVIEWEES:	Boothferry Borough Council
CURRENT STATE OF SITE:	Operational
DATE OF PLANNING PERMISSION:	1991
PREVIOUS SITE/BUILDING CONDITION:	Redundant coal fired power station
SITE SIZE:	411 ha
ESTIMATED LIFE SPAN OF OPERATIONS:	30 years
MECHANISMS TO PREVENT DERELICTION:	None

1. Keadby, five miles west of Scunthorpe in South Humberside, is the site of an old CEGB coal fired power station built in the early 1950s and taken out of service in 1982. The site area of 411 hectares is bounded on the east by the River Trent and on the west by Ealand village. Of this site area approximately 44 acres were occupied by the power station, with the majority of the remainder occupied by the coal/ash storage area, marshalling yards and conveyor systems.

2. After 1982 the power station remained on standby for a further five years, after which the site was sold to a firm of demolition contractors who removed the asbestos and most of the salvageable items such as turbines and generators. The majority of the buildings remained standing until the site was redeveloped during 1990/1. Over the period when the site was redundant, it did represent a hazard to trespassers, mainly children. (The redundant structures were also used as a 'dummy' target for RAF fighter aircraft).

3. When considering future uses for the site the owners (Energy Resources Ltd) determined that redevelopment for a gas-fired power station was an attractive option given the characteristics of the site. These include good railway connections, access to cooling water, links to the national grid and potential access to the national gas network. In addition, the previous use of the site for power production suggested good prospects of obtaining the necessary licenses for power generation.

4. Planning permission for a gas-fired power station was granted in March 1991. The proposed development was in accordance with the Humberside Structure Plan in force at that time. The final decision to develop the site was taken by the Department of Energy under Section 36 of the Electricity Act 1989. Several conditions were attached to the Section 36 consent, though none of these related to restoration of the site after the cessation of power generation. It was felt by the local authority and Secretary of State for Energy that, given the history of power generation on the site, this use would continue for some time, possibly beyond the life of the current plant. If this were not the case, the site is likely to remain in industrial use. In this case it was felt that the presence of redundant structures would not act as a significant impediment to development. A more significant constraint would be the lack of suitable road access to the trunk road network bypassing Ealand village.

5. In this case it was not felt appropriate to apply restoration conditions to the power station development. In addition, the planning authority identified administration and enforcement costs as further deterrents to using such measures. The opinion of the planning authority was that the existence of a redundant power station, despite the hazards posed by the previous coal-fired station when redundant, was not seen as a particular problem. Other planning issues such as traffic generation during construction and operational periods were seen as more important by the general public and planning authority.

2.05 MULTI-PURPOSE LEISURE FACILITY, CHESTERFIELD

INTERVIEWEES:	Chesterfield Borough Council Ecodome Ltd, Fulham
CURRENT STATE OF SITE:	Golf Course
PREVIOUS SITE/BUILDING CONDITION:	Former opencast coal site
DATE OF PLANNING PERMISSION:	1989/1992
MECHANISMS TO PREVENT DERELICTION:	None

1. ECODOME is an ambitious proposal to develop an enclosed, all-weather, multi-purpose venue with leisure, education and business tourism attractions on a site at the edge of the Peak National Park. The site was formerly an opencast quarry which was subsequently reclaimed for use as a golf course. The proposal, which has two outline planning permissions (1989 and 1992) involves the construction of various residential, hotel, exhibition and tourist facilities around parkland and retention of the existing golf course.

2. This development is of interest because it occupies a greenfield site. The nature of the development is such that the structures would not be easily adaptable to new uses should the original activities cease.

3. **In this case neither the local planning authority nor the operator felt the use of restoration conditions on the planning permission to be appropriate. The planning authority dismissed the use of such conditions on what was seen as a 'permanent' development with no identifiable lifespan. The operator felt that the site would always be attractive for some form of investment given its inherent characteristics and thus the problem of long-term dereliction would not arise. The operator also felt that financial guarantees for restoration works in the event of failure of the scheme would impose an unrealistic burden which would probably prevent the scheme from being undertaken. The operator was unwilling to discuss the scheme in any detail on the grounds of commercial sensitivity.**

2.06 COMBINED HEAT AND POWER PLANT, LEWISHAM

INTERVIEWEES:	London Borough of Lewisham
CURRENT STATE OF SITE:	Operational incinerator
DATE OF PLANNING PERMISSION:	1990
PREVIOUS SITE/BUILDING CONDITION:	Derelict and vacant
SITE SIZE:	1.6 ha
ESTIMATED LIFE SPAN OF OPERATIONS:	Ad infinitum
MECHANISMS TO PREVENT DERELICTION:	None

1. The case study site occupies approximately four acres of land north of Surrey Canal Road in the London Borough of Lewisham. The site is bounded on three sides by railway viaducts and in the south by Surrey Canal Road, which was constructed in the early 1980s in order to open up the area for development.

2. The site was formerly occupied by dog kennels associated with a greyhound stadium which occupied an adjacent site. Both the stadium and the kennels ceased to be used and were demolished during the 1960s. In 1980 a planning application was received for general industrial development on the site and outline planning permission was granted. This scheme was not implemented.

3. The site was derelict and remained in a poor state for a decade. There is no evidence that temporary, marginal or undesirable uses occurred on the site during this period and the dereliction of the site was not seen as a serious planning problem by the local authority. No action was taken by the authority to address the dereliction of the site.

4. During the 1980s Lewisham council, together with neighbouring local authorities formed the South East London Waste Disposal Group which proposed incineration as a partial solution to the lack of landfill sites for waste disposal. The Surrey Canal Road site was identified as suitable for such a facility and was identified as such in the development plan for the area. Lewisham Borough Council was involved in the consortium (SELCHP) which proposed to develop the site. Ownership of the site passed from Lewisham borough Council to SELCHP in 1990.

5. **Planning permission for the development of an incinerator / combined heat and power plant was granted in 1990. The capital cost of the scheme is estimated at £90 million. The planning authority did not seek to impose restoration conditions on the planning permission as they were not seen to be appropriate on such a development in an urban area, despite its obviously limited lifespan which is estimated to be twenty years. It is anticipated that when the present plant becomes redundant it will be replaced by a similar development.**

2.07 GOLF COURSE, RITCHINGS PARK, BUCKINGHAMSHIRE

INTERVIEWEES:	South Bucks District Council
CURRENT STATE OF SITE:	Under construction
PREVIOUS SITE/BUILDING CONDITION:	Agriculture
DATE OF PLANNING PERMISSION:	1994
SITE SIZE:	85 ha
ESTIMATED LIFE SPAN OF OPERATIONS:	Ad infinitum
MECHANISMS TO PREVENT DERELICTION:	Permission for golf course seen as mechanism to ensure long term management of site

1. The site lies within the Metropolitan Green Belt to the east of Slough. It occupies a strategic part of the Green Belt and is also within the Colne Valley Park. The site had formerly been used for a number of years for agricultural purposes, however agricultural use ceased on the western part of the site in late summer of 1990. Since then, the appearance of the site had gradually deteriorated.

2. An application was submitted in 1991 for the development of an 18 hole golf course with associated club house, together with 3 units of residential accommodation.

3. The local planning authority felt that implementation of the scheme would enhance the landscape value of the site, particularly in the degraded western part. The local authority had no objection to a golf course development in this location, being in line with policies to promote recreational uses within the Green Belt. The scheme was granted planning permission and uses subject to several conditions. This was after agreement on detailed landscaping works to be carried out in consultation with local ecological groups and consultants.

4. **Conditions attached to the permission did not relate to restoration of the site should the golf course cease operation. These were judged inappropriate in the case of a permanent permission.**

5. **The approval of this application was seen as a mechanism to ensure the long term maintenance and management of this strategic Green Belt buffer zone between Ritchings Park to the north east and Slough to the west. The approval was seen as a pragmatic approach to preventing future environmental degradation of land within the Green Belt.**

2.08 STOCKLEY BUSINESS PARK, HILLINGDON

INTERVIEWEES:	London Borough of Hillingdon Stockley Park Heathrow Consortium Ltd
CURRENT STATE OF SITE:	Business office park
PREVIOUS SITE/BUILDING CONDITION:	Local authority landfill (contaminated)
DATE OF PLANNING PERMISSION:	December 1985
SITE SIZE:	162 ha
MECHANISMS TO PREVENT DERELICTION:	None

1. The site was acquired by Stanhope Properties Plc in 1981 as an opportunity site close to the M40, M4 and Heathrow airport, albeit in the Green Belt. The site was heavily contaminated and had been derelict for some time. Stanhope Properties restored the site and constructed modern low rise office buildings. These structures, designed to be flexible to the needs of different companies, are now leased individually to blue chip organisations as office facilities. In conjunction with backing companies, Stanhope established a separate management company – Stockley Park Heathrow Consortium Ltd – to manage the office park.

2. At the time planning permission was granted, the local planning authority utilised legal agreements (S.52 – now S.106 of the 1990 Town and Country Planning Act) to obtain planning gain with regards to public access on to parts of the site including a golf course and the provision of a community park. However, the potential for future dereliction arising out of the office park was regarded as negligible.

3. The Stockley Park Consortium regarded it as extremely unlikely that the office park would ever become derelict. The structures are all modular and can be readily converted to changing demand patterns. The Consortium already has plans to refurbish the buildings at regular intervals to the standards of the day. As a commercial landlord, the Consortium's primary activity is the selling of space at Stockley Park. The site is therefore not merely an asset but the focus of its entire business. As such, there is a much stronger incentive for the Consortium to maintain the site at the highest possible standard and to adapt to changes in market demand for commercial space. This vested interest in the state of the actual site distinguishes Stockley Park from other commercial or industrial users where the site is the location of its business rather than the actual product.

4. Like any other commercial enterprise, the Stockley Park Consortium could go out of business which would leave the site as an asset to be disposed of by the Receiver. In this eventuality, there would be no restoration condition allocating responsibility for the restoration of the structures. As there are no substantial underground works and issues of contamination have already been dealt with, the cost of restoration would be comparatively low and would be offset by the scrap value of the structures involved. More importantly, the condition of the site would in all likelihood be in a much improved state compared to that preceding this development.

2.09 WEST WOOD HOLIDAY VILLAGE (PROPOSED), KENT

INTERVIEWEES:	Shepway District Council Rank Hotels and Holiday Developments Ltd
CURRENT STATE OF SITE:	Commercial forest
INTENDED USE OF SITE:	Holiday village
DATE OF PLANNING PERMISSION:	Awaiting Secretary of State decision
SITE SIZE:	121 ha
MECHANISMS TO PREVENT DERELICTION:	None

1. This application to construct a holiday village in an Area of Outstanding Natural Beauty (AONB) in East Kent is currently being reviewed by the Secretary of State for the Environment.

2. The site was identified by the applicant – Rank Hotels and Holiday Developments Ltd – through an extensive selection process involving a total of 71 sites. Kent County Council's Economic Development department assisted in this process on the basis of attracting employment to the region. Final selection was on the basis of meeting the needs of the holiday village whilst minimising any adverse environmental impact.

3. The planning issues centred around the environmental impact of the proposed development at the selected site. Nevertheless, despite the wide ranging debate relating to the importance of the natural environment at West Wood, after-use or restoration was not raised as a material issue. It is significant that nine letters from the public were received in which the need to take into account the after-use of the site was mentioned.

4. Shepway District Council did not feel that restoration conditions were warranted in this case. In their view, the holiday village was likely to succeed given the substantial investment of £100 million that the developer was putting in. Furthermore, even if the development did not succeed as a holiday village, the structures could be readily adapted for other uses such as sheltered housing or community leisure facilities.

5. Rank Hotels and Holidays Developments Ltd also had confidence in the future of their proposal. However, they acknowledged that their financial forecasts are limited to 20 years. As such, they expect to recoup their investment within 10 years of operation.

6. **The potential use of restoration conditions on these types of developments did not concern the developer unduly. The structures involved are relatively simple to dismantle and the estimated cost of clearing the site would be similar to the annual maintenance cost if the site were to remain operational ie £2.5 million. However, they were concerned that the actual standard of restoration should not be so high as to create an incentive for the local authority to insist upon restoration of the site rather than to allow conversion to another use. Experience with the older generation of holiday camps had shown Rank that sites with good locational characteristics could be sold to developers provided that a change of use would be permitted.**

7. In their negotiations regarding the West Wood site, Rank did assess the possibility of leasing the site from the Forestry Commission on a 125 year lease. Such a leasehold contract would have contained break clauses at 60 and 80 years. The operator would therefore have had the option of returning the site to the freeholder after a period of only 60 years. The implication of this type of agreement would be that the developer is prepared to restore the site in order to hand it back to the landowner at the termination of the lease.

8. **Rank were prepared to consider the use of restoration conditions on this site but did not regard them as necessary. Provided that the local authority did not infringe upon their rights to operate the site and was prepared to allow a reasonable alternative use, a restoration condition could probably have been agreed. It is notable that commercial leasehold contracts contain some of the same elements as restoration conditions.**

9. Operators are able to incorporate these liabilities in their financial plans. Furthermore, the effect of discounting will result in such conditions having at most a marginal impact on the investment decision.

2.10   BBC TRANSMITTER, BINCOMBE, NR WEYMOUTH

INTERVIEWEES:	West Dorset District Council
CURRENT STATE OF SITE:	Operational
PREVIOUS SITE/BUILDING CONDITION:	Exposed; greenfield (AONB)
DATE OF PLANNING PERMISSION:	Planning permission granted 12/2/91
SITE SIZE:	0.01 ha
ESTIMATED LIFE SPAN OF OPERATIONS:	Ad infinitum
MECHANISMS TO PREVENT DERELICTION:	None. Gentleman's agreement that when structure cases to operate, it will be removed

1. The case study highlights potential problems of changes in responsibility of land and the need to link mechanisms to prevent dereliction to the site itself rather than the operator. In the case, the local authority had a gentleman's agreement, rather than a formal mechanisms, such as a condition, to ensure the removal of structures.

2. At the end of 1990, the BBC submitted an application for a radio transmitter to West Dorset District Council. The BBC intended to lease the land from the owner to construct a 45 metre steel lattice tower.

3. The structure and local plan did not contain policies on telecommunications. The only relevant policies in plans related to protection of the AONB. These policies were set against the favourable approach to telecommunications development in the national interest, as set out in PPG8.

4. Members were in favour of the application, taking into account the guidance in PPG8. Discussions prior to a decision were held on the long term future of the site. In a letter dated 6th February 1991, the BBC gave assurances that the "proposed installation would be removed if technical developments resulted in the station no longer being needed for radio transmissions". This was agreed between the authority and the BBC but was never endorsed in a planning condition or S.106 agreement.

5. **The BBC's view was that dismantling structures was a necessity on safety (not planning) grounds. They would therefore not have objected if a condition to this effect had been placed on the application. With hindsight the authority's feels they should have secured removal of structures through a formal mechanism rather than a gentleman's agreement. Whilst the authority are confident that the BBC will dismantle the mast, they are less confident that a subsequent operator would do the same. Concerns have arisen due to the possibility of the BBC selling off its transmission function.**

2.11 BARN HILL MOTORWAY SERVICE AREA, M40 WARWICKSHIRE

INTERVIEWEES:	Stratford-on-Avon District Council Mobil Oil Company
CURRENT STATE OF SITE:	Motorway Service Area
PREVIOUS SITE/BUILDING CONDITION:	Agricultural abutting motorway
DATE OF PLANNING PERMISSION:	20 September 1991
MECHANISMS TO PREVENT DERELICTION:	No planning mechanisms. HSE regulations required limited restoration

1. Until 1992, all motorway service area (MSA) sites were determined by the Department of Transport which had a strategic policy of spacing these at 30 mile intervals. The Barn Hill site was acquired by the Department of Transport using a Compulsory Purchase Order as soon as it had been identified as a potential MSA site. In the event, four different applications went in to operate a MSA on that stretch of the M40 in South Warwickshire at two separate locations. The Mobil proposal for the Barn Hill site was eventually approved by the Secretary of State for the Environment in 1991.

2. Under the terms of the Department of the Environment Circular 18/84 relating to development on Crown Land, Stratford District Council was able only to object or support the planning application. A series of planning conditions were successfully recommended by the Council relating to environmental and operational details. At no stage of the planning process were restoration conditions proposed or the issue of potential after use considered.

3. The developer of the Barn Hill MSA, Mobil Oil, has a fifty year lease on the site from the Department of Transport. This lease requires the operator to maintain the MSA in a fully operational state and to hand it back in such a condition. Under the terms of this lease, the freeholder is responsible for any decommissioning or restoration that may subsequently be required.

4. Both Stratford District Council and Mobil argued that MSAs are strategic facilities which arise directly out of Government policy. Their future is expected to be safeguarded and secure rather than being exposed to market forces. Other petrol stations by comparison are purely competitive entities and do not have such an assured future.

5. Decommissioning for all petrol stations is partly governed by Health and Safety Executive (HSE) regulations. These relate particularly to any underground fuel tanks which must be stabilised, removed or filled when operations cease. These regulations require the operator to ensure that the site is safe to be put to another use.

6. **Mobil has accepted the use of clauses within long term leasehold contracts which relate to decommissioning at other petrol stations. Typically, leasehold agreements between the landowner and a petrol station operator will require the latter to clear any contamination that he may have caused. Provisions of leasehold agreements do not extend to the removal of structures at either the end of the lease or the operational life of the facility. Nevertheless, the stabilisation of the underground tanks under HSE regulations and the treatment of contamination ensures that the primary factors inhibiting the potential redevelopment of the site are removed.**

7. **Mobil was generally positive about the role that restoration conditions may play to deal with the physical structures. Accepting that financial planning models only extend to 20 years into the future, restoration conditions would ensure that the eventual restoration cost would be provided for in their accounts. Experience in the United States – where Mobil already make such provisions – has shown that these costs are heavily discounted and are therefore not a significant factor in making the initial investment decision.**

8. However, the use of financial guarantees was rejected as unnecessary given the track record and reputation of the operator. Arguably, the larger companies will ensure that they conform with restoration obligations largely to avoid adverse publicity. Their view was that smaller operators would find it more difficult to meet the costs of restoration after operations had ceased and would be a decisive actor in making their operations financially unviable. The effect of financial guarantees could therefore be to discriminate against smaller concerns in favour of larger organisations with sufficient resources to meet up front costs of development.

2.12 MERRY HILL SHOPPING CENTRE, DUDLEY

INTERVIEWEES:	Dudley Metropolitan Borough Council
	Richardson Brothers, Dudley
CURRENT STATE OF SITE:	Retail shopping centre
PREVIOUS SITE/BUILDING CONDITION:	Steelworks and adjoining grazing land
DATE OF PLANNING PERMISSION:	18 February 1986
SITE SIZE:	53 ha
MECHANISMS TO PREVENT DERELICTION:	None

1. In July 1981 an Enterprise Zone was designated in Dudley. This was later extended by the Dudley (Round Oaks) Enterprise Zone in October 1984. The latter zone was designated following the closure of the Round Oaks Steelworks in December 1982. Richardson Brothers, a major developer in the region's industrial land market, acquired substantial areas within the Enterprise Zone including all of the Round Oaks site in 1983 and 1984 respectively.

2. Extensive restoration work was undertaken by Richardsons to remove heavy steel structures, foundations and contamination. This work was primarily funded by the developer with no local authority involvement.

3. In 1986, Richardsons were granted planning permission to construct a 110,000 sq.m.

    (1.2 million sq.ft.) retail centre on the site. This was in contravention of the original Enterprise Zone guidelines. The shopping centre, known as Merry Hill, was opened in 1988.

4. Richardsons sold the shopping centre to Mountleigh Ltd in 1991. Subsequently Mountleigh went into receivership and attempts were made to find a purchaser for Merry Hill. The discussions at the time surrounding the proposal for a register of land exposed to contaminative processes had a negative impact on the industrial land market. Potential purchasers were concerned about the possible implications of such legislation with regard to liability in reclaimed sites such as Merry Hill, even though the proposed registers had nothing to do with liability. There were also fears that material remaining on the site could affect groundwater. However, when it became apparent that the proposals for the register were unlikely to be implemented, and when a site assessment showed that there was little or no risk of residual contamination, Merry Hill was sold to Chelsfield Plc.

5. **At the time planning permission had been granted for Merry Hill in 1986, Dudley Metropolitan Borough Council did not feel it was necessary to impose restoration conditions on the permission. Their primary concern at the time was to utilise the derelict steelworks site for local employment generating uses. Furthermore, given the scale of the ex-ante restoration required, Dudley was not in a strong position to impose restoration conditions against potential future dereliction.**

6. Richardsons felt that the Merry Hill development represented an absolute benefit to the local community in that it cleaned up the local environment and provided local facilities. Future dereliction was not regarded as a likely outcome of this development.

2.13 BROADWAY BUSINESS PARK, OLDHAM

INTERVIEWEES:	Oldham Borough Council
CURRENT STATE OF SITE:	Reclaimed and under development
PREVIOUS SITE/BUILDING CONDITION:	Derelict mixed industrial, including partially restored power station site and areas of tipping
DATE OF PLANNING PERMISSION:	Various
SITE SIZE:	54 ha
ESTIMATED LIFE SPAN OF OPERATIONS:	Ad infinitum
MECHANISMS TO PREVENT DERELICTION:	Assembly, restoration and infrastructure provision by Borough Council

1. The site occupies 54 hectares of land near the periphery of Oldham Borough, some 9 km north-east of Manchester. The site spans the Rochdale Canal and is bound on the west by a railway. It has a history of varied industrial uses for over a century. A major part of the site was formerly occupied by Chadderton Power Station, with other areas the site of cooling towers and a vitriol works. A large area of the northern part of the site was used for many years as a tip for industrial and domestic waste.

2. The site had for some time been identified by Oldham Borough Council as strategically important for employment, particularly given the poor quality of greenbelt land in the area, which makes the majority of greenfield land undevelopable.

3. The power station was decommissioned by the CEGB around 1982 and the site was purchased by a salvage company who applied for, and received, a substantial Derelict Land Grant in order to restore the land. The superstructure of the power station was removed but the foundations and contamination remained untreated. This site, together with the surrounding sites in various ownership including British Rail and the local waste disposal authority, were purchased by the Borough Council over the period 1988–89.

4. The purchase of the site, at market rates, was achieved using Council resources allocated for economic development and regeneration. Altogether approximately £10 million was spent by the Borough Council on land assembly, restoration and infrastructure provision. Some funding has subsequently been received from ERDF, DLG and from sale of land to the DOT for motorway widening.

5. The Borough Council retain ownership of the site and are selling plots of land on 999 year leases for high quality industrial users. Lease agreements drawn up by the Council include covenants which seek to control the type and quality of development on the site. These covenants refer to matters such as maintenance of the individual plots by the lessees and servicing and maintenance of communal areas by the Council. The leases state that the lessee is responsible for ensuring continued use of the site in order to maintain the overall quality of the development.

6. **Lease agreements should prevent future dereliction on the site. Where a use ceases the site should be prevented from declining into a derelict state. Where this does happen, the Council will be able to use powers under Landlord and Tenant legislation. The ultimate use of such power would be forfeiture of the lease with title reverting to the local authority. This eventually would, of course, shift the liability for restoration back to the local authority.**

Group 3: Case Studies of Derelict or Recently Reclaimed Sites:

3.01 DISUSED AIRFIELD, SILLOTH, CUMBRIA

INTERVIEWEES:	Allerdale Borough Council
CURRENT USE OF SITE:	Part derelict, part industrial use
PREVIOUS SITE/BUILDING CONDITION:	Ministry of Defence airbase/maintenance depot
SITE SIZE:	4.8 Ha
ESTIMATED LIFE SPAN OF OPERATIONS:	Nearly 30 years (in part)
MECHANISMS TO PREVENT DERELICTION:	None

1. This site was a former Ministry of Defence airbase which was last operational in 1964. Since then, a variety of industrial uses have occupied some of the larger structures on the site. These tend to be scattered around the former runways with the old accommodation and office units concentrated on a separate part of the site.

2. The overall site is now in multiple ownership with a substantial section held by one owner (including the accommodation and office units). As these structures have deteriorated, an application for private sector DLG was submitted. Since the rejection of this request, no uses have been established on this part of the site which is now in a derelict state.

3. The site is poorly accessed. Furthermore, although the local authority is seeking to attract industrial uses to the area, there is a relative over-supply of such opportunity sites. Silloth airfield is therefore a potential industrial location but only a low priority.

4. Some private sector interest has been shown in the site, with a wind farm operator seeking to locate in the general runway area. However, discussions stalled when, under the terms of a safeguarding agreement, the Ministry of Defence refused to relocate a radio beacon from the site. As such, the limited potential of the site was diminished further by an existing use which generated no benefits to the area.

5. **The local authority is not in a position to undertake restoration of the site using either Compulsory Purchase Orders or S.215 powers. In both cases, the financial burden would be too high and could not be justified against other Council priorities. Large industrial sites such as these remain in relative over-supply limiting their potential re-use, especially given the presence of dereliction, in this instance, created under Crown Immunity.**

3.02 OPEN SPACE RECLAMATION SCHEME, NORTH SKELTON, LANGBAURGH

INTERVIEWEES:	Langbaurgh Borough Council Skelton and Gilling Estates
CURRENT STATE OF SITE:	Reclaimed to open space
PREVIOUS SITE/BUILDING CONDITION:	Steep sided shale heap and mine buildings
DATE OF PLANNING PERMISSION:	Various
SITE SIZE:	Less than 20 ha
ESTIMATED LIFE SPAN OF OPERATIONS:	25 years
MECHANISMS TO REMOVE DERELICTION:	DLG and compulsory purchase by authority

1. The site had previously formed part of the Skelton and Gilling Estate and had been leased for high quality iron ore and shale extraction. The site comprised shale heap and mining buildings. In 1964 the iron ore mine ceased operating although sale of shale from the site was recorded until 1967. In the early 1970s the land on which mine buildings were located was purchased by Teesside Components, a then small engineering firm. The shale heap remained undeveloped.

2. By the mid 1970s the local authority had adopted a policy of reclamation with priority given to derelict land close to settlements. The authority therefore wished to see the site reclaimed as it closely related to the residential area of North Skelton.

3. No details are available of the discussions which occurred and whether or not the authority had sought reclamation of the site by Skelton and Gilling Estates. However, by 1977 a reclamation scheme prepared by the Council involving the retention of the shale tips and planting with pine to create public open space was approved in principle by the planning committee. At the same time the authority commenced Compulsory Purchase Order procedures to reclaim the site. There is no indication that other measures were tested prior to this.

4. **The amount of compensation for the site was not agreed until 1986 (£53,000) due to the potential value attached to the high grade shale. The Council entered the site in 1988 and reclaimed it using DLG. Final confirmation of Compulsory Purchase by the Secretary of State for the Environment was not obtained until 1993. The additional interest on the sum from the time the Council entered the land in 1988 to confirmation of the Compulsory Purchase Order in 1993 was in the region of £30,000, bringing the total cost of purchase of the site to £83,000. As the authority had reclaimed the site and retained it for public open space, under DLG guidance, no recovery of costs was required by the Department of the Environment.**

5. **North Skelton Estates had no interest in speeding up Compulsory Purchase Order process. Interest accruing was to their benefit. From their point of view, Compulsory Purchase was preferable to implementation of S.215.**

6. **The case study shows Compulsory Purchase as a means of bringing derelict land back into production and highlights the need to avoid delay in order to keep additional costs (eg interest as a result of entry to the site) to a minimum.**

3.03 FORMER SEWAGE WORKS, RODLEY, LEEDS

INTERVIEWEES:	Yorkshire Water
CURRENT STATE OF SITE:	Redundant filter beds and other plant. Part of site developed for pumping station
PREVIOUS SITE/BUILDING CONDITION:	Operational sewage treatment works
DATE OF PLANNING PERMISSION:	N/A
SITE SIZE:	Approx. 30 ha
ESTIMATED LIFE SPAN OF OPERATIONS:	1 year
MECHANISMS TO REMOVE DERELICTION:	Conversion of site to nature reserve with public access

1. The case study site is approximately 30 hectares in area and occupies a position on the floodplain of the River Aire at Rodley to the west of Leeds, near the periphery of Leeds City Council's administrative area. The site is bound to the north by the Leeds to Bradford railway line and on the other three sides by a meander of the River Aire. The site is surrounded by mixed residential and industrial uses. The site was formerly occupied by an ageing sewage treatment works, which was taken out of service in 1994.

2. The filter beds of the works remain and a small part of the site has been used for the construction of a pumping station to transfer sewage to treatment works elsewhere. While construction work on the pumping station was in progress the site was secured and protected by security guards. However, before work began the site was subject to some illegal and unwelcome activity including tipping and motor-cycling. It is expected that such uses will reoccur now that construction work and associated security protection has ceased.

3. Yorkshire Water, which owns the site, is keen to capitalise on assets which are no longer required for operational purposes. In this case, it is also concerned to prevent activities which may jeopardise its operations and may result in adverse publicity and arouse local opposition. Accordingly, the owners have sought alternative uses for the site. However, the characteristics of the site, including poor access and floodplain location, meant that no economically viable future use could be found. Nevertheless, Yorkshire Water saw an opportunity to capitalise on this asset with minimum expenditure but in a manner which derives significant benefits to the ecology, environment and amenity of the area.

4. **Yorkshire Water suggested converting the majority of the site into a nature reserve to capitalise on the developing ecology of the site while still allowing public access. This was seen as an environmentally sensitive solution to the future of the site (in line with their statutory obligations to conservation and public access under Section 3–4 of the Water Industry Act). This option would also reduce the costs of restoration compared to a more detailed landscaping exercise and is also expected to produce public relations dividends.**

5. The development of the nature reserve is still at the planning stage and Yorkshire Water are investigating potential partners in the proposal such as the Peak Park Trust, BTCV, and the conservation department of the local authority. Yorkshire Water expect to sign a management agreement with the chosen partner(s) in order to hand over the long-term management liability of the site. It is anticipated that the cost of establishing the nature reserve would be in the region of £100,000 with Yorkshire Water providing a proportion of this as seed-corn capital, with other funding being obtained by the other partners in the venture. Yorkshire Water have not sought to sell the site as they wish to retain long-term control of the land around their operational facility in the event that it may be required in the future.

6.   Yorkshire Water have very considerable land holdings and have gained wide experience of the re-use of sites which are no longer required for operational purposes. Many of the redundant assets for which alternative uses have been found are in rural locations, most notably barns. In most cases viable economic uses are found, though refurbishment and resale is usually carried out by third parties rather than directly by Yorkshire Water. Other redundant sites in the Leeds area have attracted retail and residential after-uses.

7.   This case study demonstrates the creative re-use of a site within the urban footprint which has little or no development value. The broad concern which Yorkshire Water has with landscape and asset management ensures that funds are made available for reclamation schemes such as that considered here which are not individually profit-making. The proposed reclamation will produce substantial benefits to the local ecology, environment and amenity. At the same time, the proposed scheme provides benefits to the landowner through advantageous public relations and retention of control of the site whilst reducing environmental decline but avoiding many of the direct costs associated with long-term management.

3.04 TEMPLEBOROUGH REGENERATION SITE, ROTHERHAM

INTERVIEWEES:	Rotherham Metropolitan Borough Council
CURRENT STATE OF SITE:	Reclaimed brownfield
PREVIOUS SITE/BUILDING CONDITION:	Steel stockyard with railway marshalling tracks and some mineshafts
DATE OF PLANNING PERMISSION:	Various
SITE SIZE:	4.21 ha
MECHANISMS TO REMOVE DERELICTION:	DLG

1. This site was reclaimed by the authority using Derelict Land Grant. Despite this, the site was unable to be sold on until recently due to developers' requirements for the authority to guarantee against liability for any future pollution that may occur on the site. The site adjoins the River Don. The authority is seeing a small but increasing number of similar requests on sites which they have reclaimed. The case study illustrates difficulties faced by the authority when trying to bring derelict land back into circulation.

2. At the end of 1989 the authority was approached by Swift Levick Magnets Limited, a subsidiary of a Finnish company, who wished to undertake a feasibility study with a view to purchasing the Templeborough site. To assist the company, in January 1991, the authority provided all details available of the site and its reclamation. The following month the company requested additional information from the authority including any infrastructure, contamination or site entry problems. The company also specified that if the site was purchased, it would require a warranty that the vendor would be held responsible for any infrastructure or contamination problems subsequently discovered which existed prior to the date of purchase. Effectively they required a warranty to indemnify the company against any future prosecution under the Environmental Protection Act 1990, the Water Act 1989 or any other legislation relating to the condition of the land before they acquired it.

3. After consultation with the Department of the Environment Regional Office, and other chief officers within the Council, the local authority informed Swift Levick that provision of such a warranty was not possible. The authority would adhere to the normal presumption of 'caveat emptor' (let the buyer beware) although the authority was willing for persons to enter the site to take appropriate trial boreholes. Despite this offer, the company pulled out and dropped the site for future development.

4. Little interest was shown in the site until 1993 when the authority was approached by English Estates to purchase the site. However, English Estates were also concerned about acquiring a site which had previously contained contaminants. This was partly because of the then proposed register which had raised the whole issue of land contamination and raised fears about the potential liabilities associated with owning such land. Consequently they were seeking assurances from the Council that the site did not contain anything which would constitute a 'statutory nuisance' which the Council would investigate under S.79 and S.80 of the Environmental Protection Act 1990.

5. **Rather than providing a warranty, and after consultation with the local authority's legal and administrative services, the authority were able to provide a 'letter of comfort' to English Partnerships and come to an agreement on an appropriate strategy for land purchase.**

6. **The letter of comfort specified that the Council had examined the site and found no evidence presently available to indicate the existence of a statutory nuisance in accordance with S.79 and S.80 of the Environmental Protection Act 1990. In addition, they were willing to retain the land bordering the river so as to leave a continuing liability with the Council in the event of any action from the NRA.**

3.05 BRITANNIA IRONWORKS, BEDFORD

INTERVIEWEES:	Bedford District Council
CURRENT STATE OF SITE:	Derelict
PREVIOUS SITE/BUILDING CONDITION:	Working Ironworks
DATE OF PLANNING PERMISSION:	Various recent applications
SITE SIZE:	8.5 ha
ESTIMATED LIFE SPAN OF OPERATIONS:	18 months
MECHANISMS TO REMOVE DERELICTION	None

1. This 21 acre site occupies a suburban location in Bedford, adjacent to the River Great Ouse and the London to Sheffield rail main line. Until 1993 the site was occupied by an operational iron-works. The iron works ceased operation in 1993 and the majority of the site was cleared soon after. This involved demolition of the foundry and the single storey works which comprised most of the structure. Some ancillary office buildings were retained, as was the entrance archway (Grade II listed).

2. Despite demolition of most of the structures, the site may require considerable restoration before being redeveloped as foundations remain and there is a significant contamination problem, largely in "hot-spots" throughout the site.

3. Following clearance of the site in 1993, two outline planning applications were simultaneously submitted by the owner. These were for a 17,700 sq.m. (191,000 sq.ft.) non-food retail development with associated public open space and another for a 14,000 sq.m. (151,000 sq.ft.) non-food retail scheme with 1.58 ha (3.9 acres) of residential and open space. Both of these applications were refused on the grounds that retail facilities of this nature were not appropriate or necessary in this location. The site is identified in the draft local plan for residential use. The applicant appealed but subsequently withdrew both applications.

4. A further application was submitted in 1994 for 10,200 sq.m. (110,000 sq.ft.) non-food retail scheme with 2 ha (5 acres) of residential and 4 acres of hospital development. This current application has reportedly "gone cold".

5. The local planning authority identifies the case study site as a major planning problem. The site is large and prominent, with significant problems of contamination to overcome in returning it to productive use. The site could be redeveloped as a retail park, which would involve capping the contamination and would therefore involve many of the costs of "clean-up". However, the planning authority are strongly opposed to such a use on wider planning grounds. The authority favour a residential use but the cost of restoration (difficult to assess but estimated at around £3 million) makes this uneconomic. An alternative may be to ameliorate the worst instances of contamination or cap them and convert the site to semi-natural parkland.

6. **This case study clearly demonstrates the problems associated with the polluter avoiding responsibility for their pollution. The landowners currently hold the site as a considerable financial asset, given the potential attraction for redevelopment as a retail park. The planning authority are unable to persuade the owner that the site is of little, or nil, value when restoration costs are taken into account.**

7. **The planning authority have not taken direct action to address the dereliction of the site. The costs of action taken under S.215 powers would be very high and are unlikely to be recovered from the landowner. Compulsory purchase of the site is a possibility, particularly where the site is of low, or even negative, value. On this site, however, the significant "hope value" perceived by the owner makes it very difficult for the authority to acquire it. Furthermore, the circumstances of local government finance in Bedford (which is essentially debt-free) makes financing such an acquisition difficult. In addition, even if the local authority could acquire the site for a nominal value, it would be taking on a liability which it would be very reluctant to acquire.**

8. The dereliction of the site therefore remains a problem given the economics of site value and restoration costs. The planning authority is unwilling to accept an inappropriate use on the site in order to remove the existing problem of dereliction.

3.06 DERELICT CHEMICALS SITE, WEST LONDON

INTERVIEWEES:	Site Owner/Operator
CURRENT STATE OF SITE:	Vacant
PREVIOUS SITE/BUILDING CONDITION:	Redundant chemical works
MECHANISMS TO REMOVE DERELICTION:	Industry self-regulation

1. The site is a former chemical works where buildings/structures have not been dismantled by the current site owner/operator. It is understood that there is no requirement under the original planning permission to restore/reclaim the site. In addition, there are no obligations, associated with the purchase/disposal of the site, to remove redundant structures from the site.

2. As an international company with sites elsewhere in Europe the operator has direct experience of mechanisms available in other countries. For example, in Holland responsibility for site 'clear up' is placed on the site owner/operator at the time of decommissioning/redevelopment. Disposal of a site cannot be effected without plans and specifications for the decommissioning works and this places an obligation on the owner operator to take a proactive approach to site rehabilitation. This is viewed by the site owner as being an effective mechanism for preventing dereliction.

3. The company regards decommissioning costs as part of the investment costs and would include these costs, as a part of building costs depreciated over the expected lifetime of the plant, in feasibility studies prior to development. The operator would also expect there to be some value from the sale of material on decommissioning. However, no money is specifically put aside for decommissioning and these costs are effectively treated as part of the operating/maintenance costs of the site.

4. **A forward looking approach was regarded as the most effective way of preventing dereliction whereby site owners/operators were, in effect, prevented from leaving the site without having addressed the issue of the site's condition. This relies heavily on industry codes of conduct and 'responsible' operators.**

3.07 DERELICT TOWN CENTRE SITE, CAMDEN

INTERVIEWEES:	LB Camden
CURRENT STATE OF SITE:	Derelict
PREVIOUS SITE/BUILDING CONDITION:	Bakery
DATE OF PLANNING PERMISSION:	Various
ESTIMATED LIFE SPAN OF OPERATIONS:	Early 1980's
MECHANISMS TO REMOVE DERELICTION:	None

1. The derelict structure of the old bakery is located in a mixed retail/residential area just off a major high street. The derelict structure is part of a larger development that ceased operational use as a bakery in the 1980's.

2. When the site ceased use, planning permission was given for a mixed residential/light industrial development. The application was in contravention of the plan in force at that time which designated the entire site as light industrial. However, the developer persuaded the planning authority to let him use half of the site for residential on the basis that he would ensure that a light industrial structure was erected on the remainder. This agreement was entered as a planning condition in that no part of the site could be occupied without all other parts of the site being ready for immediate occupation.

3. The developer built the housing component and sold the individual freeholds of each home. The light industrial component was never started and the original, now derelict, bakery structure remains.

4. Expression of interest have subsequently been shown in the derelict structure, especially as it is now designated on a B1 use class – permitting office development. Nevertheless, given the state of the property market and the location restriction of the site it is not a prime opportunity site.

5. **The local authority could have enforced the condition in the original planning application preventing the transfer of the residential freeholder without the prior completion of the light industrial unit. However, this option is no longer open as the developer has now moved on and the ownership of the residential units is fragmented. Alternatively, the local authority could use S.215 to provide for the removal of those aspects of the structure that have a negative impact on amenity. However, this site is not regarded as sufficiently problematic to warrant such action. The local authority would only consider such action should the public demand action at that site. Given the scale of problems in the area it is unlikely that this site will ever be high in the Council's list of priorities.**

3.08 RAILWAY SIDINGS, BEDFORD

INTERVIEWEES:	Bedford District Council
CURRENT STATE OF SITE:	Derelict
PREVIOUS SITE/BUILDING CONDITION:	Railway sidings, storage area
DATE OF PLANNING PERMISSION:	N/A
SITE SIZE:	Less than 1 ha
LENGTH OF TIME DERELICT:	Over 10 years
MECHANISMS TO REMOVE DERELICTION:	Landowner inviting interest

1. The site is owned by British Rail (Railtrack), is located adjacent to the London to Sheffield mainline and is regarded as railway operational land. The site is part of a wider area of vacant land covered in shrub vegetation and including a large redundant shed.

2. The case study site has not been used for many years and was subject to illegal waste tipping which caused access difficulties to the rail line for emergency vehicles. British Rail were concerned to prevent this tipping and sought uses for the site. The site was leased to an operator on a 6 month renewable lease and an application was received by the Borough Council for a car washing facility.

3. Subsequent uncertainty over the future of the site, in particular the possibility that it may be required for the relocation of railway sidings, led the applicant to withdraw the application and seek an alternative location elsewhere.

4. The local planning authority have previously requested British Rail to demolish and remove the redundant storage shed which is seen as a potential danger to trespassers, but without success.

5. **In this particular case, the planning authority highlighted their inability to take action against activity carried out through permitted development rights, such as exist on British Rail operational land. Similarly restoration and improvement of the site is not possible through the use of Derelict Land Grant. The planning authority therefore has very little leverage with which to seek improvement of this, or other such sites.**

3.09 WATER WORKS LAND, KEMPTON

INTERVIEWEES:	Thames Water Utilities Ltd.
CURRENT STATE OF SITE:	Landscaped following landfill operation
PREVIOUS SITE/BUILDING CONDITION:	Redundant water infrastructure
DATE OF PLANNING PERMISSION:	1992
SITE SIZE:	8 ha
ESTIMATED LIFE SPAN OF OPERATIONS:	Not applicable
MECHANISMS TO REMOVE DERELICTION:	Efforts to seek redevelopment

1. The case study site, which covers approximately 8 ha (20 acres), was formerly Thames Water operational land. The site was occupied by redundant water treatment infrastructure including an open reservoir, six filtration beds, sludge beds and a covered underground reservoir. The site is located within a narrow section of Metropolitan Green Belt between Hanworth and Sunbury and straddles the boundary between Spelthorne District Council and the London Borough of Hounslow.

2. Use of the site for water treatment ceased in the early 1980s and the owners, Thames Water, were required to bring the site, which constituted redundant operational land, into beneficial use or to dispose of it for the highest obtainable price. Accordingly, a planning application was submitted by Thames Water in 1983 for the removal of redundant waterworks structures, reinstatement of the site levels and development as a warehousing and light industrial estate with ancillary offices. Thames Water felt that the site was "unkempt, unsafe and unusable" and development would produce a positive benefit to the quality of the Green Belt in this area.

3. This application was refused at appeal on the grounds that the site is in Green Belt and the benefits to be achieved in rectifying the unkempt nature of the site did not outweigh the costs of loss of open Green Belt land.

4. In support of the application Thames Water provided details of the costs of restoration for various alternative uses. Reclamation costs associated with the industrial development proposal were estimated to be more than £300,000 (1983 prices). This was a viable proposition given the site value which would be realised in the event of industrial development. The cost of preparing the site for amenity/ recreation use with sports pitches, supervised fishing on the open reservoir and a small car park, was estimated to be less than the costs of reclamation for industrial use but unviable given the low site value for such uses. The cost of reclaiming the site for farmland was estimated to be more than one and a half times that for reclaiming the site for industrial development due to the high cost of importing topsoil and subsoil.

5. A landfill option was also explored. Here, the small income from waste disposal would serve to offset some of the restoration costs. A net restoration cost of around half that for industrial development was estimated, although the applicant believed that the small size of the site would make this an unattractive site for waste disposal.

6. In 1986 a planning application was submitted by Siemens Ltd for a 39,000 sq.m. headquarters building and landscape improvements. This application was refused, a decision endorsed by the Secretary of State at appeal, on the grounds that "the fact that the site is partially derelict is not a reason for its release from the Green Belt". This was particularly the case because the low ground levels within the site and lack of public access meant that the poor quality of the site did not compromise the open character of the site.

7. **In 1991 a planning application was submitted to Surrey County Council for landfill and landscaping. Permission was granted and the landfill scheme was implemented. The owners of the site realised that, following the failure of previous applications, landfill presented the most realistic form of development on the site. This use allowed restoration of the derelict nature of the site and also provided a moderate income during the landfill operations.**

3.10   ROADSIDE CAFE, A40 WINDRUSH, GLOUCESTERSHIRE

INTERVIEWEES:	Cotswold District Council
CURRENT STATE OF SITE:	Derelict cafe building and unmaintained hardstanding
PREVIOUS SITE/BUILDING CONDITION:	Petrol station and cafe
DATE OF PLANNING PERMISSION:	New permission granted 1994
SITE SIZE:	Less than 1 ha
LENGTH OF TIME DERELICT:	6 years
MECHANISMS TO REMOVE DERELICTION:	Granting of new planning permission for similar uses and motel

1.   The case study site is immediately adjacent to the A40 near Windrush to the west of Burford in Gloucestershire. The site comprises an area of hard-standing and dilapidated café building and smaller ancillary buildings occupying a prominent road-side position in an Area of Outstanding Natural Beauty. The site is currently used as a stopping place for heavy goods vehicles and is regularly occupied by a mobile cafe.

2.   The site formed part of the adjacent Windrush airfield used by the RAF after the Second World War. Permission was given in 1951 for the development of a transport cafe on the site. This was followed by other permissions throughout the 1960s for a cafe and lorry parking. Permission was granted in 1962 for a cafe and petrol filling station. Use continued until around 1988 and, with cessation, the site was sold.

3.   An application was received in 1989 for a 46 bedroom hotel, which was refused in 1990. An amended application was received in 1991 for a petrol filling station, restaurant and motel. Permission was granted subject to a S.106 agreement which was signed in early 1994. The legal agreement between the District Council, Department of Transport and applicant concerned highways improvements and was delayed by negotiations. The planning authority did not consider the inclusion of restoration conditions within this legal agreement. No work had begun by January 1995.

4.   The site has been the subject of considerable complaint to the local planning authority, mainly from local residents on grounds of amenity and environmental health. The local planning authority and environmental health authority regularly inspect the site but no action has been taken to mitigate the dereliction.

5.   In 1994 the planning authority sought to use powers under S.215 of the Town & Country Planning Act 1990. This was not pursued as it was deemed likely to be challenged on the grounds that the condition of the site stemmed from an activity which was not carried out in breach of planning control (under S.217 (1b)). The possibility of using Compulsory Purchase Powers was deemed too expensive by the local planning authority, particularly given the outstanding planning permission on the site.

3.11 LISTED LEADWORKS, BRISTOL

INTERVIEWEES:	Bristol City Council
CURRENT STATE OF SITE:	Renovated, further development anticipated
PREVIOUS SITE/BUILDING CONDITION:	Derelict leadworks and harbourside bonded warehouse
DATE OF PLANNING PERMISSION:	1994
SITE SIZE:	0.33 ha
ESTIMATED LIFE SPAN OF OPERATIONS:	Ad infinitum
MECHANISMS TO REMOVE DERELICTION:	Coordination of landowners in the area

1. The former leadworks is one of the buildings within the Harbourside Regeneration Area in Bristol. The docks area of Bristol has been partially derelict since the dock ceased to be operational in 1954. The leadworks was occupied by a lead-rolling company up until the mid 1960s and once the building ceased to be used it quickly fell into a derelict state. There has been no proper use of the building since 1965.

2. There was little development activity in the harbour area until the late 1970s when several storage sheds were converted to leisure uses, with the support of the City Council. To some degree these uses prevented more comprehensive redevelopment of the harbourside area, although the major constraint on development was the general economic climate and inability to find other economic uses for the site.

3. The re-use of the leadworks was particularly problematic due to the contamination problem associated with the previous use. In addition, the constrained nature of the site meant that re-use was unrealistic without the demolition of the adjacent warehouse building ('Tenbond Warehouse').

4. A solution to the dereliction of the area through large-scale redevelopment was hindered for many years by the lack of a formal planning and development framework for the area. However, in 1992 the landowners in the area came together to form a Sponsors Group in order to act together to enhance the opportunities of the location. An agreement was signed in March 1994 and now the development of the leadworks forms part of an agreed framework for infrastructure provision.

5. The City Council inherited the leadworks by default when the occupiers' lease 'fell in'. The building was subsequently listed Grade II by English Heritage, and the Council carried out renovation with funds loaned by English Partnerships. The total cost of renovation was £520,000. Renovation of the leadworks and development of the Tenbond Warehouse site behind for a multi-purpose leisure/ education facility is seen as a demonstration project for the redevelopment of the wider harbour area. It is hoped that this project, together with a Harbourside Agreement to be signed by the landowners, will lead to the comprehensive redevelopment of the area.

6. **This case study highlights the importance of cooperation and coordination among landowners in tackling local dereliction. The City Council believe that dereliction may be prolonged by uncertainty due to the lack of a coherent and agreed planning and development framework. Where landowners can be brought together to discuss mutual action and coordination of action there is real potential to tackle dereliction.**

3.12 GLOUCESTER DOCKS

INTERVIEWEES:	Gloucester City Council
CURRENT STATE OF SITE:	Part derelict /part redeveloped
PREVIOUS SITE/BUILDING CONDITION:	7-storey warehouses and canalside basin
DATE OF PLANNING PERMISSION:	Various
SITE SIZE:	14.1 ha
LENGTH OF TIME DERELICT:	Over 20 years
MECHANISMS TO REMOVE DERELICTION:	Planning brief and S.106 agreements for environmental improvement in association with redevelopment

1. Gloucester Docks, which was first developed at the beginning of the 19th century, suffered a gradual decline in activity throughout the post-war period. By the 1960s many of the warehouses had been abandoned and the owners, British Waterways Board, sought to redevelop the area. In 1966 warehouses on the West Quay were demolished. During the period of dereliction in the 1970s and 1980s various uses were attracted to the docks, largely warehousing and storage uses together with some offices and museum activities.

2. In 1980 BWB sought to demolish the Northern Warehouse to allow for redevelopment. This was opposed by the City Council due to the architectural merit of the warehouse buildings. The City Council bought the freehold of this warehouse for £1 and, using funds from English Heritage Grant and from sale and lease of other property assets, refurbished it in 1986 for use as their own administrative office. In this way the City Council acted as a catalyst to the regeneration of the docks area.

3. The City Council felt that the dock area had the potential to become a major focus for tourist and business and residential activity within the city. In March 1986 the City Council, in partnership with the British Waterways Board, produced a planning brief for Gloucester Docks and undertook marketing and promotion of the area.

4. **The majority of the site was sold to a private development company which has carried out various developments within the area. The City Council has used legal agreements in order to ensure that the general dereliction of the area is addressed at the same time as individual schemes are developed. These agreements relate, for example, to the improvement and enhancement of dockside areas adjacent to redevelopment schemes.**

3.13 POMONA DOCK SITE, CASTLEFIELDS, MANCHESTER

INTERVIEWEES:	Central Manchester Development Corporation
CURRENT STATE OF SITE:	Use abandoned and unreclaimed
PREVIOUS SITE/BUILDING CONDITION:	Working dock
DATE OF PLANNING PERMISSION:	Various
ESTIMATED LIFE SPAN OF OPERATIONS:	14 years
MECHANISMS TO REMOVE DERELICTION:	None to date

1. Pomona Dock forms the south western sector of land within the Central Manchester Development Corporation. The site has particular access difficulties. Access by boat is constrained by the low level Trafford swing bridge and connections into the city by road are poor. Ground conditions are poor; the land is unstable and the site is contaminated. The site is owned by the Manchester Ship Canal Company.

2. Structural and technological changes in the shipping industry meant that the site was no longer required. Changes included the introduction of the National Dock Labour Scheme which streamlined the workforce, and the shift in the industry from use of small ships to large containers (which were unable to pass under the swing bridge). The site was therefore abandoned in the mid 1970s.

3. Some low grade uses were located on the site until it was designated an Enterprise Zone, and later incorporated into the Development Corporation area. Despite these development incentives the site has remained derelict to date. There is little prospect of private sector development as the site has negative equity. There is also a plentiful supply of less constrained sites within the Corporation area.

4. The Corporation now aim to develop the site as a Public Open Space. They see no short term hard end use market for the land.

5. The Corporation's view is that very little could have been done to prevent the site from becoming derelict. Although the principle of requiring the Ship Company to restore the site might have been a good one, it would be unworkable. Problems at the site are extensive and any surface restoration would be cosmetic. It would be unreasonable to require the Ship Company to resolve access issues which are the most constraining aspect of the site. Equally it would be unreasonable to require them to remove contaminants caused by industry which had long since disappeared.

6. The relationship between the Ship Canal Company and the Development Corporation is relatively good. If a Notice similar to a S.215 were served on the Company then this relationship could be jeopardised. The scope for negotiations would be reduced.

7. The Development Corporation envisage that a good way forward is to enter a tripartite partnership between the Corporation, the Ship Company and a private developer. This would enable the cost of redevelopment (either for soft or hard end uses) to be shared.

3.14 MILLS REFURBISHMENT, OLDHAM

INTERVIEWEES:	Oldham Borough Council
CURRENT STATE OF SITE:	Occupied by Council-run managed workspace scheme
PREVIOUS SITE/BUILDING CONDITION:	Redundant single-storey turn-of-the-century weaving shed
DATE OF PLANNING PERMISSION:	Various
SITE SIZE:	Less than 1 ha
ESTIMATED LIFE SPAN OF OPERATIONS:	Ad infinitum
MECHANISMS TO REMOVE DERELICTION:	Purchased and renovated by Borough Council

1. There are estimated to be around 80 late nineteenth and early twentieth century multi-storey cotton mills within the Borough of Oldham. At Victoria Street, Chadderton three mills (one actually a single storey weaving shed) were occupied by a locally important manufacturing company which was seeking alternative premises. The Borough Council provided the company with alternative premises elsewhere and the three mills became vacant between 1990 and 1991.

2. The three mills were purchased by the Council and the single storey mill was restored by the Borough Council at a cost of around £1.7 million using funding from ERDF, Urban Programme and other sources.

3. The re-use of the two multi-storey mills was more problematic. The Borough Council devised a scheme for the re-use of one, but this was only realistic if car parking could be provided, which entailed the demolition of the other mill. In 1993 English Heritage were requested by conservationists to list the buildings. The Borough Council argued that listing would effectively prevent any realistic future use being found for the mills. The most architecturally interesting mill was eventually listed while the other was demolished.

4. The Council used this example to highlight the potential problem of listing effectively contributing to dereliction by limiting the options for the economic reuse of redundant buildings. The Council have successfully prevented listing of several redundant mills in the Borough but feel that many more have and will continue to become derelict because private landowners may not have the wherewithal to oppose the listing process.

3.15 CHAPELHALL BRICKWORKS, LANARKSHIRE

INTERVIEWEES:	Monklands District Council Lanarkshire Development Agency D & J McKenzie Ltd
CURRENT STATE OF SITE:	Contaminated, vacant site
PREVIOUS SITE/BUILDING CONDITION:	Brickworks (also ironworks and coal mine)
SITE SIZE:	34.3 ha
ESTIMATED LIFE SPAN OF OPERATIONS:	Nearly 10 years
MECHANISMS TO REMOVE DERELICTION:	Sale of capital stock

1. The old Chapelhall Brickworks is a large industrial site just north of the main M8/A8 Glasgow-Edinburgh road. There is an extensive history of workings on the site including coal mining, ironworks and brickworks. The site has been derelict since 1985.

2. The site was acquired by the present owner after the brickworks closed as part of an overall deal relating to a range of plant and property belonging to the operator. The present owner removed all the plant from the site and undertook basic restoration works involving the removal of the structures. Additional works were carried out in conjunction with the local authority regarding to the levelling of the old spoil heaps from the mineral workings. Vehicle access points to the site have been blocked to prevent fly-tipping and illegal occupation. At present the site is not a visual eye-sore despite the large area that it covers. Pedestrians still have access and there is evidence of it being used by the local community as a substantial area of open space. Nevertheless, there is extensive contamination on the site which has not been treated.

3. The local authority in conjunction with the Lanarkshire Development Agency has attempted to bring this site back into use. Given the plentiful supply of good industrial sites in the region, this site has been identified as a potential outdoor recreation facility as well as a small industrial park. A scheme was developed which included a provision for open-cast mining the remaining coal reserves on the site to offset the restoration cost. However, the remaining restoration cost of between £1 – 3 million could not be justified by the public authorities.

4. The landowner does not have any plans to redevelop the site and is awaiting a suitable offer which reflects what he regards as its excellent commercial potential. As such he is still expecting to realise around £275,000.

5. Arguably, the landowner is not imposing any externality costs upon the area in that the site is not impeding development as neighbouring properties. Similarly there is only a limited opportunity cost in terms of alternative uses that could be made of the site. Given that the public sector is not able to finance the current net restoration cost, increasing local authority powers would not change the situation. The consultants' view is that the use of a tax on the holding of derelict land could prompt the owner to revise his price and encourage him to market the site more actively. However, it is unlikely that a charge would be justified in this case as the landowner has undertaken some restoration work maintains the site in a generally tidy state.

6. The cost of restoration at this site could rise to £7 million – a cost that the local authority could not fund nor expect to recover from a landowner with no other interests in the property. Tackling dereliction of this order is therefore likely to remain an issue which will need to be dealt with through imaginative schemes combining public and private funding rather than direct action against the landowners.

Practical Issues Relating to a Tax on the Holding of Derelict Land

The Detailed Taxation Option

H1   This appendix analyses the detailed issues relating to the option of placing a tax on the holding of derelict land. The topics discussed include the setting of the tax amount, the administration of such a tax and the possibility of tax avoidance strategies.

Setting the Tax Amount

H2   This proposed tax would be primarily geared to creating appropriate incentives and penalties to prevent dereliction rather than to raise revenue. The incentive effect requires that the tax be set equal to the external cost of dereliction to the rest of the economy. Clearly it would be practically impossible to assess this cost, especially where many parties were affected and no price could be put on the cost of dereliction to each individual. Essentially, there is no market for dereliction and no simple exchange value exists. More complex use values involving subjective valuations of dereliction determine the "true cost" of dereliction.

H3   Consequently, another method of assessing the tax would have to be used. To derive an efficient pricing of the externality cost, note would have to be taken of the incentive effect as well as the administrative cost of arriving at the tax charge for each derelict site.

H4   There are two approaches to setting a price on the external cost of dereliction:

a)   Value-linked Assessments

The tax could be set as a percentage of the present use value of the land. Similar in approach to the council tax or the old rates system, this approach relies upon a positive value of the land in order to obtain revenue. As the market value for derelict sites would generally be negative (when restoration costs are taken into account), this would not generate a positive tax liability. As such, there would be an incentive to hold land in a derelict state to ensure that the present use value remained negative to minimise this tax liability.

Alternatively, the tax could be levied on the previous use value of the site. In the majority of cases, the site would still have planning permission relating to this use. As such, the previous use would represent one possible alternative use of the site. The previous use value of the site could also be readily determined by examining the accounts for when the site was still in use. The drawback of this valuation method is that the site may no longer be viable in this previous use with the failure of that particular activity being the cause of the subsequent dereliction. As such, the previous use valuation could penalise the landowner excessively by placing a value on this site which could no longer be realised even after restoration.

b) Flat Rate Charge

Another method of levying a charge could be on the basis of a flat rate per unit area of derelict land. This rate could be set nationally, regionally, locally or even by previous use type. For example, heavy industrial dereliction could attract a higher rate than redundant rural sites. Similarly, the flat rate could be indexed over time so as to place a higher rate on long term dereliction.

There are precedents for both value-linked and flat rate charges. The former would be directed at the underlying value of the land in an alternative use. The latter option is more akin to the Uniform Business Rate (UBR) in that it would levy a flat rate (on area rather than value) – although this could be varied across certain aspects of dereliction. The flat rate system would be relatively straightforward to administer at a national level whilst it could still be adjusted to local conditions. The previous use valuation is more complicated in that it depends on individual site valuations increasing the administrative burden as well as introducing scope for disputes relating to site assessments.

Although neither of these approaches attempts to define the external cost of dereliction at an individual site, the setting of a tax would provide an incentive to avoid dereliction. The flat rate charge would allow the tax amount (and therefore the size of the incentive) to be tailored to policy objectives. As such, policy, rather than the external economic cost, would set the price of dereliction. Certain types of dereliction could therefore be penalised more heavily than others.

The flat rate charge approach does not allow for extensive local variation beyond the physical assessment exercise. Local discretion in setting the charge could actually result in substantial degrees of variation between different parts of the country and therefore undermine the "level playing field" upon which areas seek to compete. The flat rate charge is therefore the most effective method of using the fiscal system to create efficient incentives which are consistent with a national policy relating to the prevention of derelict land.

Administration of the Tax

H5   The appropriate level of government to administer a tax on derelict land remains open to debate. Given that the tax base – ie land that is derelict – would require detailed local knowledge, local authorities would clearly have a role to play. However the administrative costs of each local authority operating its own system for assessing, levying and collecting this tax would be very high.

H6   A possible option may be to combine the efficiency of central tax collection and enforcement with local input. The system would be administered centrally (levying and collection) with local input regarding the actual assessment. There would thus be similarities with the existing UBR. Local authorities would be responsible for maintaining their register of derelict land which would have to be revised as sites moved in and out of dereliction. These would be undertaken in line with national guidelines defining which criteria should be used and how sites should be assessed.

Tax Avoidance

H7   In the event that the tax burden outweighed the use value of the site, rational landowners may seek to transfer the site out of their ownership. At one level, this is exactly what the tax would be trying to encourage: the transfer of land from uses with low social benefit to uses with a higher social benefit.

H8   Nevertheless, some owners may wish to retain control over the site whilst seeking to minimise or avoid the tax liability.

a) Overall Tax Liability

If a tax on derelict land was levied nationally, then it would form part of the overall tax liability of the landowner/ operator. As such, the tax on derelict land could be offset by any losses that the operator is making elsewhere. Similarly, the effect of this tax could be negated through the creative use of capital allowances and other provisions.

Nevertheless, measures to minimise overall tax liability generally only defer liability and should therefore not affect the long term impact of this tax. The only long term avoidance of this tax would arise if the taxable entity made continuous net losses for tax purposes across all operations or achieved losses through the availability of group loss relief.

b) Separate Charge

The tax could be dealt with on the basis that it did not form part of the general tax liability and could not therefore be offset by losses or tax allowances. In essence, such a charge would form a direct cost of holding land derelict regardless of the ownership or organisational structure. The economic incentive impact would not therefore be diluted within the general tax burden of larger enterprises and would remain effective for smaller operators making net losses.

If the original landowner cannot use tax minimisation strategies, he may seek to avoid the tax liability of the site whilst still retaining ultimate control – for example by transferring the site to a property investment company for which the derelict site is the only asset.

The Inland Revenue would still be able to press for payment of the tax liability either from other parts of the accounting group or by petitioning for bankruptcy. Although these actions could delay payment of the tax liability the Inland Revenue would eventually be able to press for payment from the ultimate owner.

Avoiding the tax whilst retaining ultimate control over the site would therefore be extremely complex and may involve overseas transactions. Given the legal and financial penalties that could be incurred, it is unlikely that tax avoidance would be a major issue should this tax be introduced.

Printed in the UK for HMSO
Dd. 301207 C7 11/95 9385 3151